1

Dear Reader

This book was translated into English with DeepL Translator pro.

The information and data contained in the book relate to the European Union, with a focus on Austria and Germany.

However, the functions of today's monetary system are the same throughout the world and differ only by small variations.

EU specific names and processes, which are not necessarily known in English-speaking countries, are explained at the respective places in the book.

I hope the translation by DeepL pro is good enough and meets the requirements of the English-speaking reader.

If you find gross errors in the translation, I would be very pleased to receive feedback from you.

Many thanks and enjoy reading.

Daniel Müller

d.mueller(at)dezentrale.at

About the author

My name is Daniel Müller. I was born in Switzerland in 1967 and I now live in Austria for 25 years. I am a self-employed event technician since 1997 and have established a second mainstay in recent years with the installation of photovoltaic systems. For 4 years I have been intensively involved with the Blockchain technology. A few months ago, I passed the exam to become a Blockchain Professional. I would like to pass on this knowledge via deZentrale.at.

Interest in the economic and monetary system has existed for more than 15 years, but has inevitably picked up during the 2008 crisis.

To explain this in more detail, I must go back a little and briefly explain the Austrian social security system.

A self-employed person in Austria pays his social security contributions on the basis of taxable profits.

Normally, tax returns are submitted by September of the following year at the latest. That is Sept. 2020 for the year 2019.

It can happen that the social security does not receive the data from the tax authorities until a few months later and that these data are not included in the calculation of the advance payments, in our example for 2021. This means that the possible additional payments would not be offset until 2022.

As a result, larger amounts may have to be set aside for social security payments.

Before 2008, you could simply leave these amounts on your account and offset inflation with bank interest. After 2008 this was no longer possible, as bank interest rates slipped to zero. If you left the reserves on the account, you made a loss.

This prompted me to attend several seminars of the Vienna Stock Exchange Academy to learn the basics of stock exchange trading. I now parked part of my reserves in shares, bonds and options. It was never about getting rich, but only about inflation protection, so everything was invested very conservatively. It worked to a large extent.

In spring 2016, I came into contact with cryptocurrencies for the first time and was enthusiastic about the new technology. At the beginning I only recognized to a rudimentary extent what potential it had, but the deeper I went, the more I became aware of the potential.

During this I came across the Austrian School of Economics. Of course, I dealt with it intensively and built up a useful knowledge and understanding. Since I like to see the whole picture, I also read Marx and Engels as well as J.M. Keynes. This allows me to compare the individual economic concepts and, at least in principle, to judge them. Whereby such an assessment can only be subjective.

I hope that this book will give you some experiences and views and enable you to draw your own conclusions.

Sense and purpose of this book

For many people, the monetary and financial system is a book with seven seals. Far too complicated, boring and therefore uninteresting. With this book I try to explain the monetary and financial system. It is not as complicated as it be always told. Most of it is based on common sense and does not contain mathematical formulas or fancy technical terms.
The reason why it is repeatedly claimed that everything is so terribly complicated is only because this claim is intended to conceal the elites' actions. As long as nobody understands how the system works, the elites can do whatever they want and continue to enrich themselves on the shoulders of the taxpayers.
I have tried to present the connections as simple as possible, in order to bring the connections closer to the absolute layman.
Maybe I will manage to arouse your interest and you will start to get a little closer to the subject.

Much of this book was written during the Covid-19 crisis in March 2020, when stock markets fell by around 30% in 4 weeks. Central banks cut their key interest rates further and the economy is flooded with trillions of new money (1 with 12 zeros). It looks like we are stumbling into a new financial crisis, which is not surprising and has been predicted by some, much smarter people for quite some time.
Of course, the blame for this crisis will be put on the coronavirus. In reality, the coronavirus is not to blame for this crisis, it just mercilessly exposes the weaknesses of our system, which is built on debt.
After reading this book, it should be clear where the problems really lie.
In the third part of the book, I outline a possible approach, it is up to us to change something and push for a system change. Every crisis is also an opportunity, let us seize it.

You will hear our elites say in the coming months that they now know what needs to be changed. They will create new regulations and laws to keep us citizens under control (cash abolition, etc.), always under the guise of financial stability, money laundering, terrorism financing and new because of Covid-19.

Be critical, after reading this book you should know why.

For easier understanding the book is divided into three parts:

Part 1

In the first part, the origins and history of money are examined.

What are the characteristics of money and what must money be able to do.

I will also briefly examine the various forms of money to give the reader a rough overview. It is important to know what used to be in the past because this is the only way to understand what is going wrong today.

Part 2

In the second part, I look at the prevailing fiat currency system as we use it today. Where the problems lie and why it cannot work.

Part 3

In the third part I present my vision of a possible future. In my vision, crypto-currencies, such as Bitcoin, play a leading role.

I will also look at ways in which we can regain some freedom.

All three parts are divided into chapters, so that later reference to individual topics is easy.

Table of contents

Part 1:

Part 2:

Fiat currencies

Part 3:

Before we get into the subject, I would like to clear up two misunderstandings. You do not have to understand these misunderstandings immediately, but it is important to keep them in mind. In the following chapters you will understand exactly what it is all about and by the end of the book I hope these misunderstandings will have been cleared up.

1st misunderstanding

The numbers on my account show my wealth

Almost all people believe that the numbers in bank accounts show their prosperity. The higher the number, the wealthier the owner. Unfortunately, this is not true. In the following I will try to explain what real wealth is and it has nothing to do with numbers on accounts.

Suppose you have bought a nice, fresh potato to prepare lunch with. If you cut this potato in half, you get two halves, so far, so logical. If we think about this further, it means that each of these halves is worth half a potato.

Now let's go a step further and cut these two halves in half again. Now we have four quarters, which also means that each piece of potato is only worth a quarter potato. Are you still with us? I think so.

We can now cut this potato further into smaller pieces, say a hundred small cubes. In this case, one piece of this potato would be worth 1/100 of a potato.

In this example, we can see that the smaller we cut this potato, the less value the individual potato piece has. However, the number of existing potatoes has not changed. If you put the two halves back together after the first cut you will still get a whole potato and if you put the hundred potato pieces back together you will get only one potato.

The prosperity, i.e. the number of potatoes you own, has not changed, your prosperity has only been divided into smaller pieces.

If we now apply this knowledge to the numbers on your account, it should be clear that these numbers only represent the potato pieces and not the number of potatoes in your possession.

Prosperity arises on the other side, in our example with potatoes. Your prosperity has only increased if you own two potatoes.

Now we take the step into the real world. On the one hand, we have our numbers on the account and on the other hand we have the goods, products and services that the economy, i.e. the shops, dealers, car manufacturers, etc. offer us for sale. The economy is in a way the potato of our example.

If we now assume that a fairy godmother doubled our figures on the account overnight, but economic performance remained the same, there was no change in prosperity, economic performance was only cut into smaller pieces.

When economic output rises and new products and services are offered, but the numbers on our account have not grown, then prosperity has increased.

2. misunderstanding

The Euro, Dollar, Swiss Franc, etc. is money

As we will see in the next chapter, money must have a decisive quality. Money must conserve the value of work done. This means that a service already rendered should not be worth less in the future. In English one speaks of: "Store of Value", in German Wert = (Value), Speicher = (Store), in the whole of the Wertspeicher.

The euro, the dollar, the Swiss franc and whatever they are called, cannot do it!

A clear distinction must therefore be made between money, which is a store of value, and currency, which is not a store of value.

Part 1

What is money?

In addition to the physical characteristics listed in the following chapter, money has another, more philosophical characteristic. Money stores a performance. I am not talking here about the intrinsic value of money, but about the performance of its owner. To illustrate this, here are two small examples:

When salaries are paid at the end of the month, the amount paid out reflects the performance and work of the previous month. In the euro area, for example, this could be 2000.- euros. These 2000.- euros therefore represent the value of the work done.

From the point of view of an entrepreneur who produces bricks, for example, the monthly production of, say, 10,000.- bricks at 5.- euros each, i.e. 50,000.- euros, would be the equivalent of the work and energy invested.

It is important to understand that these euro amounts should preserve the work done and can be exchanged at a later date for food, luxury goods, services, etc. Thus, by using the euro, it should be possible to exchange work done for food, luxury goods, services, etc., i.e. for benefits from other people.

Basic characteristics of money

In this chapter we will take a closer look at 8 basic characteristics of money.

What must money be able to do to be used sensibly?

On the one hand, money serves as a **means of exchange and payment.** This means that money is generally accepted to pay for goods and services. This requires that all market participants (buyers and sellers) trust the medium of money and its value.

Furthermore, the money must be **durable.** Which means nothing other than that the money should not go mouldy, should melt, rot or otherwise dissolve. As far as durability is concerned, metals, gemstones, shells, etc. have proven to be suitable.

Another property of money is its function as a **unit of account.** This property allows market participants (buyers and sellers) to define prices for goods and services. For example, one litre of milk costs 1.20.- euros. If products and services can be defined by a price, the possibility of comparing products and services automatically arises.

Divisibility is another property that money needs. It must be possible to divide money into smaller pieces without losing its original qualities. Metals can easily be divided, for example by sawing or melting them down. With animals, it looks a bit different, if we divide them they lose an important quality, namely life.

Fungibility or **comparability** is the next important property. Fungibility means, for example, that every €1.- coin has the same value. If I want to buy something for one euro, it must make no difference which 1.- euro coin I pay with.

Rarity is another property that money should possess. Gold, silver, precious stones, etc., are rare, whereas sand, soil or pebbles, for example, do not possess this property.

The **intrinsic value** is another criterion which, at least in the past, was important. The intrinsic value is the material value of money or the effort that has to be made to make this money available. In English one speaks of "Proof of Work".

This describes the following circumstance:

When we hold a lump of gold in our hands, this lump of gold is proof that someone has used work and energy to get this gold out of the soil. If no work and energy had been put in, we would not be able to hold this nugget of gold in our hands because it simply would not exist.

Stability of value/purchasing power retention is the next property that money must possess. Imagine you receive a salary of 1000 euros for their work. But they don't want to spend the money for a month. It would be stupid if after one month, for your 1000.- Euro, you could only consume goods and services worth 900.- Euro.

This would mean that the value/purchasing power of your 1000.- euros would have fallen by around 10% within one month.

Another point is **transportability.** It makes little sense if I need a truck to transport my money to the vegetable market, just, so I can pay for my weekly shopping at the market.

So, now we have illuminated the properties of money, and we will see in the further course of the book what all these properties are like.

The barter trade

Bartering worked and still works to some extent today, in that goods were and are exchanged for other goods. For example, if a hunter needed a new pair of shoes, he would go to the shoemaker and offer him a freshly hunted hare in return. If the shoemaker had a use for a freshly hunted hare, there was nothing to prevent the trade.

It only got silly when the shoemaker didn't need a rabbit, but perhaps fresh leather for new shoes. The hunter could then go to the tanner and offer him the hare for leather. When the tanner agreed to the trade, the hunter finally got his shoes after all.

If we now compare the hare with the characteristics of money, we see that only a few characteristics are represented in this hare:

Acceptance:
Only to a limited extent. I have to find someone who wants the rabbit.
Durability:
This is not given as the hare decays in a few days
Unit of account:
Only very limited
Divisibility:
With dead rabbits limited possible
Comparability:
No because not every rabbit is the same size or weight
Rarity:
Only conditionally
Inner value:
Existing, as labour and energy have been invested in hunting
Value retention:
No. See durability
Transportability:
Basically fulfilled

The precursors of money

In this chapter we will take a brief look at the precursors of money.

As we have seen with the example of our hunter and his hares, bartering can sometimes be difficult. Bartering usually works well enough in small communities such as clans, tribes or small villages, but if you want to trade with the neighbouring village or more distant communities, bartering quickly reaches its limits.

From these circumstances the precursors of money, the so-called commodity money, emerged.

Commodity money is defined as all goods that can be exchanged. This can be gold, silver, precious stones but also domestic animals such as chickens, sheep and goats. Cigarettes or tobacco can also be used as means of exchange.

Let us now look at commodity money and its properties.

Acceptance:
Yes, at least for the acting partners
Durability:
In principle yes, e.g. somewhat limited for live animals
Unit of account:
Yes
Divisibility:
Yes, only not possible with live animals
Comparability:
Only conditionally
Rarity:
In principle yes, otherwise acceptance would not be given
Inner value:
Available
Value retention:
Restricted for plants and animals
Transportability:
Basically fulfilled

The coins

Coins were first minted in Lydia (the territory of present-day Turkey) some 2650 years ago.

The coins had the decisive advantage over commodity money that they contained an exact quantity and quality of the metal used. For example, 10 grams of silver or 1 ounce (31.1 grams) of gold. The material and weight were guaranteed by the issuer. Due to these characteristics it was now possible to engage in international trade, provided that the metals used were also used as means of payment in other countries. Gold and silver have spread almost worldwide as accepted means of payment.

The coinage system of that time was by no means only in state hands. Nobles and also private persons could mint coins, but needed, at least in part, permission from the government.

Let's take a look at how the coin performs in our comparison:

Acceptance:
Largely no restrictions
Durability:
Yes
Unit of account:
Yes
Divisibility:
fulfilled, by minting coins of different values
Comparability:
Yes
Rarity:
Yes
Inner value:
Yes
Value retention:
Yes
Transportability:
Met, at least for smaller amounts

Paper money

Paper money arose from the fact that it was sometimes a bit cumbersome to carry large sums of money with you. Especially when trading with other cities or even other countries, it was not wise to carry around kilograms of silver or gold.

It was therefore decided to deposit their gold and silver in a warehouse or in a bank. The bank guaranteed the security of the deposits and issued the customer with a receipt for his stored gold and silver. The bank charged a fee for guarding the deposits; this was the banks' actual business model.

If the customer wanted his deposits back, all he had to do was show the receipt and his gold and silver would be returned.

Soon it was no longer gold and silver that was used to pay for goods and services, but bank receipts.

Over time, this was even possible across national borders, as banks also accepted receipts from other trusted banks. The gold and silver stocks were then, based on the receipts, balanced among the banks.

Now what about paper money and its properties:

Acceptance:
Largely fulfilled
Durability:
Yes
Unit of account:
Yes
Divisibility:
Yes
Comparability:
Yes
Rarity:
Yes
Inner value:
Fulfilled, since gold and silver is underlaid

Value retention:
Yeses
Transportability:
Yes

The gold standard

As we have seen in the previous chapter, the receipts were issued by private banks. This means that only receipts from trusted banks were accepted, which again is an important part of a free market economy. If the issuing bank was not trustworthy, for whatever reason, the receipts were not accepted. As a result, the banks tried to do business in a serious manner in order to survive.

With the introduction of the state gold standard and later the central banks, monetary sovereignty was returned to the state. Under the gold standard, the government had to have gold reserves at its disposal and issued banknotes based on existing gold holdings.

The gold standard enabled the owner to exchange his banknote money for gold at any time at a fixed exchange rate.

This posed some problems for the state. Firstly, the state was not able to expand the money supply without increasing its gold and/or silver reserves. Secondly, the state lost precious metal reserves when importing goods from abroad. For example, if the imported goods were paid for with dollars, the exporting country, for example France, could always exchange the dollars received for gold at a fixed exchange rate. As a result, France could print more banknotes, since it now had additional gold from America, and America had to collect banknotes to ensure 100% coverage of the dollar.

Here again the comparison to the basic properties:

Acceptance:
Yes
Durability:
Yes
Unit of account:
Yes
Divisibility:
Fulfilled, through the publication of different note values
Comparability:
Yes
Rarity:
Yes
Inner value:
Fulfilled, because backed with precious metals
Value retention:
Yes
Transportability:
Yes

Bretton Woods System

The name Bretton Woods refers to a place in the United States. In 1944, several leaders, 44 to be precise, met there to negotiate a new international monetary system.

At the end of the event the following key points were agreed upon:

The US dollar was again pegged to gold at $35 per fine ounce of gold.

The remaining currencies were pegged to the dollar at a fixed exchange rate.

The United States thus held gold to cover its dollars and the other countries held dollars to cover their currencies.

The American citizen was no longer able to exchange his dollars for gold. Dollars were only exchanged for gold bars in large quantities and the exchange of coins was abolished.

In August 1971, the President of the United States, Richard Nixon, unlinked the US dollar to gold.

Since then, all currencies worldwide have been so-called fiat currencies.

Here again a small overview of the properties:

Acceptance:
Yes
Durability:
Yes
Unit of account:
Yes
Divisibility:
Yes
Comparability:
Yes
Rarity:
Yes
Inner value:
Fulfilled, at least partially, as all currencies are linked to the dollar are pegged
Value retention:
Yes
Transportability:
Yes

Part 2

Fiat Currencies Basics

As we have seen so far, all previous monetary systems had an intrinsic value. Work and energy had to be invested, either to dig for gold or to hunt rabbits. Furthermore, all types of money had fulfilled the function of storing value.

The fiat currency system works the other way round, it is based on debt and, as we shall see, it loses its function as a store of value. So from now on we are no longer talking about money but about currency.

J. P. Morgan, a founding member of the Federal Reserve and investment banker, described it at the time as follows:

"Gold is money, everything else is debt!"

And here is a bon mot from Henry Ford, the founder of the Ford Motor Company:

"Actually, it is a good thing that the people of the nation do not understand our banking and monetary system. If they did, we would have a revolution before tomorrow morning."

With these two quotes in our ears, let us now take a look at how such a fiat currency system works. Of course, there are differences from country to country, but by and large the procedures are identical.

Commercial banks and central banks

Let us first look at the central banks. The central banks issue the central bank currency. The central bank currency comprises all the notes, coins and reserves of the commercial banks that are held in the accounts of the central bank. Only commercial banks and governments have accounts with the central bank, all others have accounts with commercial banks. Commercial banks include, for example, Deutsche Bank, Commerzbank, Santander, UBS and what they are all called, in short, all banks serving individuals and companies.

Central bank currency arises when the central bank, in our example the European Central Bank (ECB), buys a government bond from Italy. The government bond costs €20 million. These 20 million euros are credited to Italy's central bank account. If Italy wants the 20 million in cash, it is printed by the central bank.

The problem with the whole thing is that the ECB has no euros to buy government bonds. As soon as the 20 million appears in Italy's account, the ECB has invented 20 million euros and created it from absolute NOTHING.

Another task of central banks is to provide currency to commercial banks so that they can issue loans.

In simple terms, this works as follows:

The central bank grants a commercial bank a loan of, say, €1 million. This million also comes out of nowhere and is simply credited to the bank's account. The commercial bank can now issue loans to the value of 100,000,000, in words: one hundred million euros. All commercial banks are obliged to keep reserves of 1% of the total amount of the credit in the Central Bank's account. The level of the required reserves may vary and is not the same for all central banks. In 2019, the ECB is required to hold a reserve of 1%.

Now, of course, the question arises how the commercial bank can issue almost 100 million euros in loans? Well, that is actually simple, the commercial bank simply invents the 100 million.

Suppose a company needs a loan of 10 million euros for the construction of a new warehouse. The commercial bank grants this loan and credits the 10 million to the company's account. Again, money is created out of nothing because the bank only needs to have a reserve of 1% (as of 2019 ECB) on its account with the central bank (100`000.-), the remaining 9.9 million are simply created out of nothing. This form of currency is called book currency or bank currency and can only be drawn from commercial banks.

Commercial banks may also grant loans based on any customer deposit. If, for example, Max Mustermann has an amount of 1000 euros in his account, the bank can grant loans to the equivalent of 100,000 euros and, of course, these 100,000 euros are also simply drawn from nothing.

To take the madness a little further, the following example:

Mr A obtained a loan of 10,000 euros from his bank for a new car. This means that the bank which granted the loan must have a reserve of 100 euros at the ECB.

Mr A now goes to the car dealer of his choice and buys a new car with the 10,000 euros. The car dealer in turn brings the 10,000 euros to his bank and pays the amount into his account. The car dealer's bank now has the possibility to issue loans worth 1,000,000 euros based on the 10,000 euros.

As we have seen, in today's system, the Euros, Dollars, etc. are created from nothing and are always based on debt.

The above examples and procedures may vary in different countries, and economic circumstances may also cause changes in the approach. The above examples are assuming that banks have a credit rating of AAA. This means that the banks offer the best rating and therefore the greatest economic security. If the rating is less good, banks must show a percentage of the loans as equity. The worse the credit rating, the higher the percentage of equity they must have or the fewer loans they can issue.

That is why our currencies are called fiat currencies. Fiat is Latin for: "Let it be or let it arise". In the Bible, "fiat lux" means "let there be light".

As we can see, the basic characteristics of money have changed completely. Gold and gold-backed currencies have always needed a service, be it labour, energy or both, to be created. The property of money as a store of value has also disappeared, more on this in the chapter on inflation. Nowadays, debts are incurred to create new notes, coins and book money. This approach of course brings with it some problems, which we will discuss in the next chapters.

Yes, here too is a brief overview of the properties:

Acceptance:
Complies, as prescribed by the state as legal currency
Durability:
Yes
Unit of account:
Yes
Divisibility:
Yes
Comparability:
Yes
Rarity:
with restrictions, see inflation

Inner value:
Not available
Value retention:
Not met, see inflation
Transportability:
Yes

Inflation

Formerly

At the time when the minting of coins was still in private hands, there were unfortunately already black sheep who wanted to enrich themselves fraudulently. A common means was the addition of inferior metals. The weight of the coin remained unchanged but the quality of the metals used was reduced. This means, for example, that a coin worth one ounce of gold still weighed one ounce but only contained 20 grams of real gold, the rest could be copper, for example. This of course was tantamount to devaluing the coin.
By way of illustration:

3 ounces of gold (~ 90 grams) yielded 3 coins.
If 10 grams of copper (3 × 10 grams) were added to each coin, the total weight would be 120 grams (90 grams of gold + 30 grams of copper).
From these 120 grams, however, 4 coins could suddenly be minted.
This means that for every third coin the mint received another "free" one.

This of course had an impact on the population.

When private mints started to devalue their coins, these coins were no longer accepted by the people and other coins were used. Or, the coins with the lower value were used with the new value, until the mint overdid it with the devaluation and the coin was no longer used.

In the above example, the coin would only be valued at 20 grams of gold and therefore have less purchasing power than a coin with a whole ounce of gold. Market participants therefore reacted to this situation within a very short time and either gave the "bad" coins a lower value or exchanged them for another coin. This is a classic example of a free market economy.

The State interferes.

Again and again, states issued their own coins and claimed coin sovereignty for themselves. The argument put forward was the fight against bad coins from private mints, i.e. the addition of inferior metals.

Once the State had taken over minting sovereignty, the State laid down by law that the State coins were accepted on the territory and had to be used to pay taxes and fees.

This state coinage sovereignty spread relatively quickly to other states and is still valid in this form today.

Unfortunately, however, it turned out that states also began to devalue their coins. This actually always happened when a war was being fought. In order to finance the immense costs of a war, the now state-owned mints mixed inferior metals into their coins to mint more coins and thus finance the wars.

However, this procedure had consequences for the population, as the national coins had to be accepted, now by law. The population no longer had the option of simply not accepting the coins and switching to other coins. In addition, taxes and fees could only be paid with the government coins. This in turn put further pressure on the population and forced them to accept the state coins, as otherwise they could not pay their fees and taxes.

We can see that in the case of a non-government minted coin, only the high-quality coins were in circulation and the bad ones were sorted out. When the state took over the minting sovereignty, the opposite happened, the good coins were taken out of circulation and hoarded, while the bad ones were issued as quickly as possible. This is a superb example of state intervention that did exactly the opposite of what was originally planned.

Today

The elites, such as politicians, central bank directors and economists, tirelessly point out that it must be possible to adjust the quantity of currency (e.g. the euro) at any time to match economic performance and, if necessary, to support the economy with more currency units. This is very difficult to achieve with a gold-backed monetary system. To bring more money into circulation, more gold reserves are first needed, which naturally stands in the way of spontaneous government intervention.

But what is inflation and how does it come about?

Inflation is nothing more than the artificial inflation of the currency amount and the resulting devaluation of the currency.

In earlier times, coins were mixed with inferior metals, so they contained less gold than originally intended.

This saved gold on the other hand and made it possible to use it for other inferior coins. This meant that the same amount of gold could be used to mint more coins. As a result, the money supply was inflated (Inflare Lat. for inflating/swelling), thereby devaluing the money.

Here again the example from an earlier chapter:

3 ounces of gold (~90 grams) yielded 3 coins.
If 10 grams of copper (3 × 10 grams) were added to each coin, the total weight would be ~ 120 grams (90 grams of gold + 30 grams of copper).
From these 120 grams, however, 4 coins could suddenly be minted.
This means that for every third coin, the mint received another one "free", thus artificially inflating the money supply.

This example shows that the size of inflation was relatively easy to determine. It is the ratio between the gold and the metal added.

Inflation worked similarly in gold-backed monetary systems. For example, if at the time of introduction a $20 note was backed by an ounce of gold, we speak of a 1 to 1 coverage. This means that the owner of a 20 dollar note could exchange his note for 1 ounce of gold at any time and vice versa. However, this exchange was repeatedly prohibited by the state, usually just before or during a war.
This allowed the state to devalue its currency by suddenly using 1 ounce of gold to cover 30 dollars (1 to 1.5). This artificially inflated the currency again, causing it to become inflated. Again, it is relatively easy to determine inflation; it consists of the ratio of the quantity of currency units to gold reserves.

Determining inflation in a pure fiat currency is a little more complicated because the currency is not backed by anything.
To explain the determination of inflation in fiat currencies, we have to make a small diversion via prices.
Any kind of inflation reduces the value of each currency unit (see the potato example).
If gold covers 1 to 1, assuming again 20 dollars, which corresponds to one ounce of gold, the price of an ounce of gold is exactly 20 dollars. If the currency is now inflated and 1 to 2 cover is introduced, an ounce of gold suddenly costs 40 dollars. Which means that the individual dollar is now only worth half that amount. In this extreme example we would have 100% inflation.
We therefore see that inflation always causes a rise in prices, whether it is a pure gold currency, gold backed currency or fiat currency. When the currency supply is inflated, the value of the individual coin automatically decreases and prices rise.

Now that we know that inflation is always expressed through prices, we can look at how inflation is measured in fiat currencies.

A virtual basket is usually used for this purpose. This basket contains around 650 goods and services that are regularly consumed by the population. (as of 2018 Germany). It includes various foodstuffs, energy (oil, electricity, gas), clothing, luxury goods (tobacco, alcohol), leisure time, etc. In short, goods and services of daily use.
To determine the inflation rate, the cost of the basket is measured monthly. If the price of the shopping basket has risen, the price increase, in percent, is called the inflation rate.
This example is only intended to illustrate the basic way in which the inflation rate is determined. In practice, different baskets of goods are used and technological progress (better computers, better equipped vehicles, etc.) are also taken into account in the calculation.

But this calculation using the shopping baskets also has considerable disadvantages. The main disadvantage is that the consumer is seen as a group and not as an individual. A vegetarian does not care if meat prices have risen or not because he or she does not consume meat. A convinced cyclist cares very little whether fuel prices have risen, but a taxi driver does care. So, we see that this form of calculation is insufficient.

A much broader approach is to compare total economic growth (not just a basket of goods) against the quantity of currency. This results in a much wider dispersion and the examples of the vegan, cyclist and taxi driver would not be so far apart, i.e. would show a real average.

For explanation:

In order to have prices as stable as possible, which is the aim of all central banks, the volume of currency must grow at the same rate as the economy grows. This means that if the economy grows by 2%, the volume of currency must also grow by 2%. If the volume of currency grows by more than 2%, we have inflation and prices will rise by the same amount as the volume of currency has grown by more than 2%.

Put more simply:

Increase in currency volume in percent minus increase in economic growth (GDP gross domestic product) in percent. These data are provided by each central bank and show real inflation.

The following table shows very impressively how the figures really look for Germany

Money supply M3		Growth	True inflation	Official inflation
Jahr	Geldmenge M3	Wachstum	wahre Inflation	offizielle Inflation
2012	+6,95%	+0,7%	+6,25%	+2,0%
2011	+4,84%	+3,0%	+1,84%	+2,5%
2010	+0,53%	+3,5%	−2,97%	+1,2%
2009	+3,0%	−4,9%	+7,9%	+0,4%
2008	+9,5%	+1,3%	+8,2%	+1,3%
2007	+11,13%	+2,5%	+8,63%	+2,3%
2006	+8,53%	+3,0%	+5,53%	+1,6%
2005	+7,42%	+0,8%	+6,62%	+1,5%
2004	+5,86%	+1,6%	+4,26%	+1,6%
2003	+8,1%	−0,1%	+8,2%	+1,0%
2002	+7,18%	+0,1%	+7,08%	+1,4%
2001	+5,6%	+0,8%	+4,8%	+1,8%

Source: FOCUS Money/ Bundesbank/ ECB

If the result is a positive number, we speak of inflation, if it is a negative number we speak of deflation (more on this later) and if it is zero, we speak of absolute price stability.

The question now is, of course, why governments and central banks consider inflation so important and desirable and why they are trying to keep annual inflation at 2%. The simple and worrying answer is that inflation is the expropriation of citizens and is a hidden tax.

Two conditions must be met in order to carry out this expropriation of citizens:

Firstly, the currency monopoly must be in state hands and secondly, this currency must be the only legal tender allowed by law.

Both conditions have long been met in all countries.

But how exactly does this expropriation work? To clarify this, we need to look at two terms: "close to money and far from money". Close to money are banks, states and corporations, while far from money refers to the poorer sections of the population. All other population groups are somewhere in between, with entrepreneurs being closer to money and white-collar workers and blue-collar workers being farther from money. Put more simply, the easier it is to get a large loan, the closer you are to money.

In the first example, let's look at what happens when a group takes out a loan:

Group XY wants to build a new production plant and needs a €100 million loan for this purpose. This 100 million is created out of nothing by a commercial bank and increases the amount of currency in circulation by exactly this 100 million. The group is now having its new production plant built at a cost of 100 million. So far, so good. But as we have already seen, inflation causes prices to rise. The price increase does not happen overnight, but it takes time for inflation to take hold. This means that in future consumers will have to pay more for their weekly shopping, in our example the effect of the new 100 million.

Let's just assume that the inflation rate caused by the new 100 million is 2%. This means that consumers will have to pay 2% more for their weekly purchases. But it also means that the value of the new production plant has increased by 2%, so it is now worth 102 million. The products which are now produced in this very new production plant have also become 2% more expensive.

From a worker's point of view, the following has now happened:

He will still receive the same salary, but will be able to buy fewer products and services, as the purchasing power of his salary has fallen by around 2%. (1.961% to be precise)

So, we see that the purchasing power has moved from the worker, who can afford about 2% less in real terms, to the group, as the new production plant has gained 2% in value and the goods produced have also become 2% more expensive.

The poorer sections of the population are even worse affected. The worker normally receives an annual salary increase to cushion inflation. But people who are dependent on social welfare or pensioners, for example, do not receive this pay rise every year and thus suffer most from the rising prices.

Now let us look at what happens when the state takes out loans:

First we need to take a brief look at how states get their euros, tax revenues now put aside.

A state auctions off government bonds. Financial institutions such as banks, insurance companies, investment companies, etc. participate in these auctions. The winner of the auction is the one who charges the least interest, i.e. who costs the state the least.

When banks buy government bonds and thus grant the state a loan, the amount is naturally created out of nothing. Other participants in the auction have the opportunity to sell their government bonds to the central bank, which of course also pays for the bonds with money created out of nothing. During crisis, central banks also buy up government bonds directly, including those with money created from nothing.

If countries drive inflation by borrowing, through government bonds, for infrastructure or for social projects, the consequences are even worse.

Let us again take 2% inflation as an assumption. For infrastructure projects, they too will increase by 2%, but this will be accompanied by a 2% increase in revenue for fees and government services such as motor vehicles registration, waste charges, etc., as these prices are of course also rising. If the worker gets his salary increase, the state also takes action again because higher taxes are due in percentage terms.

Meanwhile, the government debt burden is reduced by around 2% (1.961% to be precise), given the 2% nominal increase in the volume of currency. In other words, let's take the debt burden as 100 million. This amount does not change, it is the sum that has been paid out and has to be paid back by credit/government bond (we leave the interest out). If we make a diversion via the purchasing power, it should be easier to understand. Let us assume that in 2018 this loan was taken out for 100 million. This means that in 2018 this loan had a purchasing power of 100 million. With an inflation rate of 2% per year, this 100 million will only have a purchasing power of about 98 million in 2019, so inflation has reduced the debt level. (the two percent is not quite correct, the purchasing power is reduced by 1.961 %. The nominal value of the credit would have increased by two percent with the same purchasing power 102 million)

If you think it all through, it turns out that any gift from the state, be it an increase in social benefits, tax cuts or similar election promises, hits the poorest of the population hardest. Since the state always has to borrow for these promises and thus drives up inflation. The only one who benefits from such gifts is the state and never the population because they pay the bill.

To top all this hocus-pocus off, it must be clear that this game is based on real inflation and not on the figures published by the government, which are calculated from the shopping baskets.

For the worker, this means that although he or she receives a salary increase (inflation compensation) of about 2% per annum, the actual inflation is much higher (about twice as high on average)

This means that the purchasing power of the ordinary worker is shrinking by a few percent every year. All these correlations are the reason why the middle class has long been disappearing and the gap between rich and poor is widening.

If we remember the first chapter "What is money" we know that money should store our work performance in order to be able to exchange it for goods and services at a later date. Seen from this point of view, inflation is nothing other than the retrospective devaluation of the work done. I think that you get into a considerable explanatory difficulty when you explain to an employee that the work she did last year is worth less today.

Deflation

Deflation is the opposite of inflation. Deflation reduces the quantity of currency and prices fall. Or, the economy grows faster than the currency volume, which has the same effect. Deflation is feared by the states and the elites because it causes a reversal of purchasing power towards the poorer ones and debt can no longer be inflated away.

While inflation "encourages" the population to spend their money as quickly as possible, the exact opposite happens with deflation. Since the population knows that purchasing power is constantly increasing, larger investments such as a new car, new kitchen, etc. are postponed into the future. As a result, the economy is supposedly deprived of Euros and producers and service providers make less turnover and profit.

Let us now take a closer look at this situation. It is quite true that in the event of deflation, the population tends to save money and postpones major purchases into the future. But it is also the case that investments are still made, and if the car is broken, a new one has to be bought. Even the purchases for daily life must be made now and can hardly be postponed into the future. At the same time, it is also the case that producers can produce at lower prices, since purchase prices are falling there too. Only companies that were already on the brink of collapse are now going downhill faster because the debt burden is higher in case of deflation and is no longer sustainable. From this point of view, a phase of deflation could be understood as a market shake-out, as only the solid companies will survive. For the population, especially the poorer ones, this would result in an improvement of their situation. Apart from the fact that some products and services would no longer be available because the suppliers would have to file for bankruptcy.

The biggest losers would be the states, as the hidden tax would disappear and the debt burden would increase.

This purifying effect could also lead to a situation where states and governments finally start spending more carefully and not wasting taxpayers' money senselessly. (Berlin Airport, Stuttgart 21, Gorch Fock, to name but a few)

Interest

In this chapter we will take a closer look at interest rates. First of all, we are interested in what interest rates actually are.

Interest is nothing more than a price. The interest rate is the price that a borrower can use euros today that he will earn in the future.

Let's say I want to buy a new washing machine today for 500.- euros. But I do not have the 500.- euros I need and therefore need a loan. In one year I would have saved up the 500 Euros without any problems, but I cannot wait a year because I need a new washing machine today. So, it shows that the credit of 500 Euros is nothing else than that I can use the 500.- Euros I would have in one year today. The price for this service is the interest.

From the point of view of the lender who has the 500.- euros, the interest rate is the price he charges because he cannot spend his 500.- euros until a year later.

In this example it is clearly evident that the lender has the 500.- euro. So he has renounced or saved something, otherwise he would not have the 500.-.

If we start from private individuals above, the same applies to banks in a gold standard. These banks also had to earn the money before they could lend it, or they lent their clients' money and shared the interest income with the clients. In either case, the money had to be there and belong to someone.

Another important task of interest rates is risk assessment. Suppose you lend someone 1000.- for one year.

If you know this person well, the interest rate will be lower because you are sure you will get back the 1000.-.

If you don't know the person you will charge higher interest because you are taking a higher risk, because you cannot be 100% sure that you will get your 1000.- back.

Against this background the question arises why banks charge interest in a fiat currency system. After all, banks have not saved or renounced anything, they just type a number into a table and create the 500.- out of nothing. It is neither their Euros nor did they have to pay anything for it. The same goes for central banks, why do commercial banks have to pay interest when they take out a loan from the central bank. Also, the central bank has not obtained the euros by giving up or saving them, but invents them while booking the euros into the commercial bank's account.

In a fiat currency system, interest is nothing more than a licence to oust the customer.

Now let's take a quick look at how the lending business works in a Fiat system. The bank types a number into a table and the amount appears on the borrower's account. There are two things to note.

Firstly, the loan increased the money supply (inflation) and secondly, the interest due was not created. The inflation effect should be clear but the second circumstance deserves closer examination.

Imagine an island with 10 inhabitants. On the first of January a stranger enters the island and gives each of the ten inhabitants 100 euros. The stranger gives the inhabitants 100 euros each to put at their free disposal, on condition that they get 110 euros each back in a year. He therefore charges an interest of 10%. So, there are exactly 1000 euros in circulation on this island. But the problem is that the foreigner wants a total of 1100 euros back in one year. In the best case, nine islanders can repay their loan with interest and one of them has only 10 euros left.

Nowadays, the tenth island resident would simply ask for a new loan to pay off his debts.

So he pays debts with new debts. This is the usual procedure of states, banks and corporations. All others have to file for bankruptcy. It is often pointed out that in the real world, not on our small island, the economy is constantly growing and generating new values. That is why the interest rate problem is no longer dramatic.

But what is forgotten is that these new values are also based on debt. The whole debt-based system and interest rates are forcing the population to work more and more.

To pay the interest, I have to take the money away from someone else, but to do this, I have to work more, otherwise someone else will take the money away from me.

Central Banks

Now that we have a rough idea of how our dominant monetary system works, let us take a closer look at the central and commercial banks.

Let us first take a closer look at the tasks of a central bank. The central banks are responsible for issuing the national currency, keeping prices "stable" (inflation rate of around 2%), providing liquidity to the economy through the commercial banks and, in some cases, supervising the banks.

Now we will take a brief look at the tools used by central banks, the only ones of interest here being price stability and the supply of money to the economy.

On the one hand, the central bank sets the key interest rates. These are the interest rates that commercial banks must pay when they borrow currency from the central bank.

Secondly, central banks buy up debt (government bonds, corporate bonds, etc.). Buying up debt depends on the financial situation of the country and the economy. In times of crisis, the central bank buys almost any kind of debt and in stable times it usually buys only government bonds.

Now that we also know what the central banks are using, we are looking at what effect these funds will have.

Key interest rates

As we already know, the base rate is the interest rate that banks have to pay when they borrow currency from the central bank. When lending, banks charge the borrower the base rate plus the interest that the bank itself charges. Therefore, if the base rate is high, the interest rate for the borrower will also be high, which in turn means that fewer loans will be issued because the interest burden on the borrower is high. So, if fewer loans are taken out, fewer new euros will come into circulation and inflation will be reduced. On the other hand, if the banks store surpluses at the central bank, they will of course receive higher interest rates. This, in turn, means that savers are more likely to deposit their euros in a savings account than to spend them, since they also receive higher interest rates from the bank. In this case, the banks pass on part of their interest gains to the saver. This savings incentive also means that fewer euros are in circulation and therefore inflation is reduced.

With a low-key interest rate, the opposite happens. The loans become cheaper because the interest rates are also much lower.

This means more loans are taken out and more currency comes into circulation.

In addition, saving is no longer worthwhile and the Euros are spent rather than put on a savings account.

The idea of low-interest rates is supposed to boost the economy because there is more currency available to spend and it is no longer worth saving.

There is only one catch: the more currency there is in circulation, the higher the risk of inflation.

The next step is the negative interest, which means that if I take out a loan I have to pay back less than I borrowed, or, if I park Euros in my account, I have less in my account at the end of the year, because I am paying negative or penalty interest.

What exactly happens when we live in a negative interest rate environment?

The banks can borrow currency from the central bank for zero percent interest. The idea behind this is the same as with low-interest rates, only much more radical, the currency is to be spent and the economy is to be boosted. Saving now makes no sense at all, and the banks also avoid storing surpluses at the central bank because they too have to pay negative or, better said, penalty interest.

Incalculable side effects

It is now the case that around 75 per cent of the loans granted are not spent on the construction of a new production facility or on new equipment and machinery, so they will not flow into the real economy and do what was actually intended by the central banks, namely strengthen the economy.

Instead, the loans are used in the financial sector to speculate on the stock markets or invest in real estate. Especially in the real estate market, the effects are disastrous, as investors are prepared to pay ever higher prices and thus drive real estate prices to undreamt-of heights, which in turn is reflected in constantly rising rents. The increased rents in turn make it almost impossible for the poorer sections of the population to rent a flat, as they simply cannot afford the rents.

Not only investors are to blame for the rising rents, but the problem lies with the central banks, which are flooding the markets with ever cheaper money and thus creating incentives to buy more and more property on credit and speculate with real estate. If the interest rates for loans were at a reasonable level, such a thing would not happen because such speculations could not be financed.

Another problem is the rural exodus, more and more people moving to the cities, where normal market forces are at work, the more demand, the higher the prices. This is a policy failure. Poor transport links between rural areas and the cities, resulting in few economic settlements in rural areas, which creates few jobs and drives the population to the cities.

Other price drivers are pension and retirement insurance. Pension and annuity insurance companies endeavour to invest policyholders' deposits as securely as possible and thus minimize the risk.

In the past, such insurance companies invested in government bonds issued by various countries, real estate and similarly secure forms of investment. Now the insurance companies are faced with the problem that German government bonds are sold at minus interest rates, but they still have to generate profits to achieve the guaranteed interest rates in the policies. This drives insurance companies more into the real estate market and into risky asset classes.

Again, the European Central Bank is solely to blame for this situation. The same game is being played in other countries and continents. Inflation is not even considered in this whole drama.

The example of Berlin is another failure of politics. About 15 years ago Berlin sold all the flats and houses it owned for ridiculous prices and today everyone is wondering why there are no cheap flats.

(The city of Berlin sold about 200`000 flats to private companies from the year 2000 on. After the flats are sold, the rents increased by about 20 %)

Rental price caps are introduced and expropriation is mentioned. The perpetrators of the problems, politics and the central bank are being ignored as far as possible, as elections are imminent. In short, the institutions that have completely screwed up and are responsible for the problems are now blaming the private sector. Unfortunately, Berlin is not an isolated case.

Another side effect in the financial sector is the so-called buybacks of listed companies on credit. A buyback describes the repurchase of own shares. Buying back own shares reduces the number of shares available on the stock exchanges. This in turn leads to a rise in share prices and therefore increases the value of the company. Don't forget that this artificial increase in the value of the company is also based on debt.

Another problem caused by this cheap money, which is the last example, are the so-called zombie companies. A zombie company is a company that has not made a profit for more than three years, so the rough definition. About 15 percent of all companies in the 14 leading industrial nations are considered zombie companies. (according to BIS, Bank for International Settlements)

A zombie company is kept artificially alive by cheap loans. But this ties up capital unnecessarily, which is not available to new companies. This indirectly slows down progress and innovation. In a normal interest rate environment, these zombie companies would have disappeared from the market long ago, but thanks to the existing interest rate environment, they are still in the market and are constantly multiplying.

But the problem is not only with the zombie companies alone, it also affects the banks that give loans to the zombie companies.

When the next economic downturn hits and these zombie companies go down the drain, we will see an unprecedented number of unemployed people and some banks will also be dragged down by these bankruptcies. Again, the most vulnerable will suffer most from the mismanagement and greed of our elites. But the main evil, our monetary system will of course be defended, after all it lives quite well by expropriating the population.

The low or negative interest rate environment also eliminated an important feature of natural interest rates. It is no longer possible to make a risk assessment based on interest rates.

All the incalculable side effects, and this was only a small selection, we have considered without considering economic performance. Unfortunately, however, the economy has also become gloomier recently, meaning that it is no longer growing as strongly as it did a few years ago. In concrete terms, this means that economic growth in the euro area has halved between 2017 and 2019 and with Covid-19 it will get even worse.

Bond purchase

Central banks have the possibility to buy government and corporate bonds. This is another way in which a central bank can put more currency into circulation and support the economy.

Since November 2019, the ECB has been buying up government bonds again, in the amount of 20 billion per month. With this action the ECB is trying to dampen the economic downturn.

We have now seen the how central banks try to keep prices "stable" and support the economy. We have also seen that these measures generate side effects that were never planned, and we now also know that despite the efforts of the central banks (in our case the ECB), economic output has fallen.

What we have left out of the considerations is inflation. All these measures are based on the multiplication of currency, in our case the euro.

Commercial banks

We look at the problems that arise for commercial banks when central banks cut interest rates and even declare negative interest rates (penalty interest).

One of the banks' main sources of income is interest rate transactions. The banks lend money to other banks. In a normal interest rate environment this can generate a decent income. However, the lower the base rate, the lower the interest income.

Let us recall the negative interest rate environment currently prevailing. The central bank is trying to put money into circulation by offering commercial banks loans at zero percent interest rates. This enables the commercial banks to grant cheap loans, which is intended to boost consumption and thus strengthen the economy.

But now that the banks also have to pay penalty interest when parking currency at the ECB, new problems arise.

Until recently, commercial banks passed on the negative interest rates to companies at most. This means that when companies parked Euros at banks, they had to pay penalty interest. Meanwhile, some banks in Germany have started to pass on these penalty interest rates to normal customers. Especially new customers of a bank have to swallow the penalty interest.

All in all, dark times for savers.

But if we follow the idea further we will come to a point where nobody really wants to go.

So if banks start passing on the negative interest to their customers, this could lead to customers closing their accounts and finding a bank that does not pass on the penalty interest to the customers. This would give a short-term advantage to the banks that pass on the penalty interest to their customers. The advantage would be that the banks would have to manage fewer deposits and would therefore have fewer deposits with the ECB and would therefore have to pay less penalty interest but could also issue less credit.

But the problem that this creates is not really more pleasant. The outflow of customers' money worsens the banks' balance sheets and suddenly business figures look even worse.

This in turn could lead to a deterioration in the creditworthiness of the banks concerned, which could result in a loss of confidence. This loss of confidence could lead to the remaining customers to close their accounts and suddenly, we have a bank that needs to be rescued. The small advantage has thus relatively quickly proved to be not so great.

But what happens to the banks that did not pass on the negative interest rates? They will have to rethink their business model rapidly because more customer deposits also mean more deposits with the ECB and therefore higher penalty interest rates. It will not take long and these banks will also pass on the penalty interest to their customers. Since from a certain point on all banks will have to pass on the penalty interest, I assume that this will lead to a nightmare for every bank. Customers will try to clear their accounts and put the money back under their pillows.

However, as we already know, banks do not have nearly as much cash as they need to pay out all their customers. What follows is pure chaos.

Of course, the government will intervene beforehand and restrict cash withdrawals both at the counter and at ATMs. Certainly some banks will simply not open their doors any more so that nobody can withdraw money. Any Greek or Cypriot can give you further information, they have already played the game about 10 years ago.

All the DFIs (Draghis funny ideas) have put the European Union in a rather awkward position, but this is being swept under the carpet by governments, central bankers and other experts. (*Mario Draghi was the president of the European Central Bank until 2019*)
The bad thing is, it gets worse:

Life insurance and pension funds

Many people think that pensions are reasonably safe. The amounts paid into life insurance policies are also a good investment in the future.
I'm not so sure about that.
Both the pension insurance companies and the life insurance companies have to invest their deposits in a profitable way. Unfortunately, it is not possible to leave them on accounts because of penalty interest. Government bonds are also difficult, as interest rates there are also close to zero or even negative. Real estate would still be an option, but unfortunately the real estate market is already overheating due to the cheap loans, so much so that a considerable loss potential is to be feared there as well. So, what should the insurance companies do? Surely there are "still" investment opportunities that yield some profit, but at least the pension funds are limited in this respect, as they are only allowed to invest in supposedly safe forms of investment. (real estate, government bonds, etc.).

We now want to let inflation play a part in these considerations as well.

If the insurance companies and pension funds can generate a return of four percent, which I doubt, they will lose two percent of that to inflation, but as we have already seen, inflation is much higher, which means that the insurance companies and pension funds will at best not make a loss but in any case not a profit.

Another problem, which is often concealed, is the instalments that are paid in. If we assume a fixed amount that is paid in monthly, say 100.-, this means that in one year we will have paid in 1200. But since the value of this 1200.- is also subject to annual inflation, the purchasing power of this 1200.- dwindles annually by the value of inflation.

In 20 years' time, the purchasing power of 1200.- will be only about €750.- in the first year.

This also means that the amount you have saved looks very nice by numbers, but the purchasing power of this nice number has dropped by almost a quarter.

The following diagram is intended to illustrate the effects.

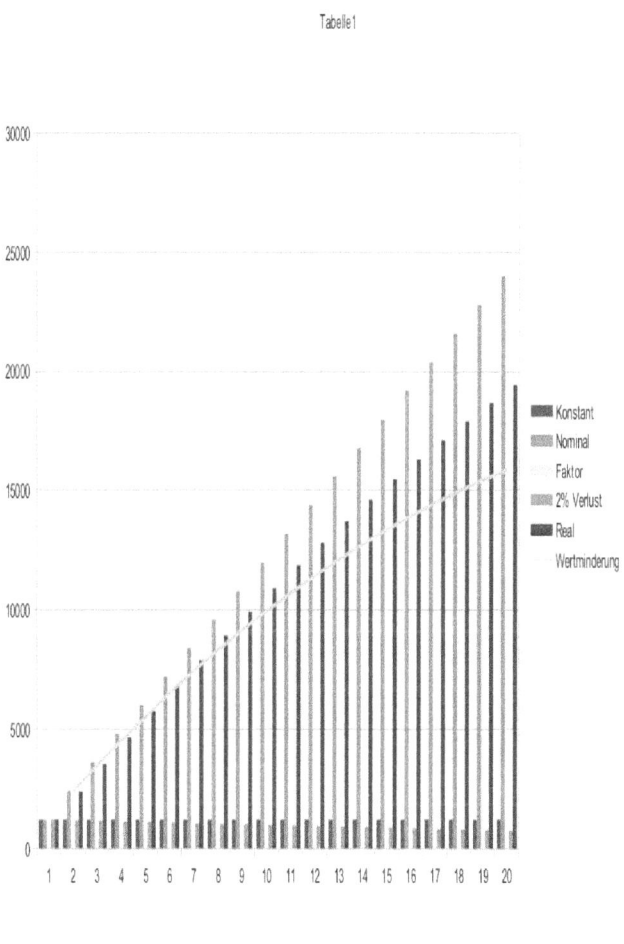

Source: *deZentrale.at/ Daniel Müller*

The "nominal" columns show the 1200.- nominal paid in annually without inflation = 24`000.-

The "Real" pillars show the 1200.00 paid in annually with a loss of purchasing power of 2% = 19'440.00

The "Wertminderung" line shows the complete loss of purchasing power over 20 years without interest gains = 15,889.00

If the insurance company manages to earn 2% interest, the "Wertminderung" line will align with the "real" pillars, as the savings will not decrease.

However, the "real" pillars are not affected by this, as the loss of purchasing power of deposits remains

As icing on the cake, the age pyramid should be brought into play for a short time. This shows that fewer and fewer working people should pay for more and more pensioners.

Now everyone can take a moment to consider whether pension and life insurance is as secure as they keep telling you.

Another not inconsiderable question you need to ask yourself is the following:

Will the euro or the insurance company still exist 20 years from now?

This is, at least in the present day, a pretty daring bet.

Special case Euro

In this chapter we will take a closer look at the euro. I can promise you that after this chapter you will see the euro with different eyes.

Let us start with the original idea in a highly abbreviated form:

The euro is designed to facilitate trade within the euro area and reduce or eliminate currency costs such as exchange charges, exchange rate differences between national currencies and transaction costs.

The first problems with the euro, however, arose when it was introduced. The reason was the valuation of the individual national currencies, or in other words how high inflation was in the individual countries. There were countries with relatively high inflation, which means that these countries increased their currencies more than their economies grew and therefore devalued their currencies. On the other hand, there were states which had inflation under control and therefore had stable currencies.

The problem was now the national exchange rates against the euro. It was now necessary to combine undervalued or real and therefore stable currencies with overvalued currencies and to unite them in the euro. This inevitably favoured some countries and disadvantaged others.

In the case of the respective national currencies, the states were able to revalue their currency up or down at any time. With the euro, this is no longer possible because all countries use the same currency, which brings us to the next problem.

Let us assume that a state has stable, not artificially generated, economic growth based on innovation and real efficiency. Such a state has different requirements for monetary policy than a state where economic performance is weak.

If monetary policy raises interest rates, which would be good for the state with the economic growth, the state with the weak economy will in return slide into recession because this state would need low interest rates to boost the economy. Since the euro does not allow for individual states to be dealt with, monetary policy in the euro area is always a complete mess and will never work.

A further problem lies, once again, in the false incentives that are being created. The euro creates a kind of joint liability of all euro states. If one state gets into trouble, Greece, Italy, Spain etc., the other states have to pay directly or indirectly. The various rescue packages are borne by all euro states or rather all European taxpayers.

These rescue parachutes create the false incentives mentioned at the beginning of this article. Why should a state "pull itself together" and work in an economically sensible way, if something goes wrong, the other states have to take the blame.

A next detail in this context is the EU's financial stability rules. An EU country should not have more than 3% new debt and 60% public debt as a percentage of gross domestic product (GDP).

Failure to comply with these rules could result in heavy fines. Unfortunately, not a single infringement has been sanctioned and there have been and still are many.

Greece is by far the leader in terms of government debt, with just under 180% (12.12.16), while Estonia is in last place with a government debt ratio of around 9.5 %. (as at 12.12.16). However, it is alarming that only 12 out of 28 states (as of 12.12.16) have a debt ratio below 60%. Germany 68%, Austria 84%, France 95% to name but a few. Since 2016, government debt has tended to fall somewhat, but this will change abruptly again with Covid-19.

Another institution in the EU is the EU budget pot. All countries contribute to this pot and the EU redistributes the money to the member states in the form of subsidies and similar grants. Now, after the Brexit, there are ten countries that pay in more than they get back, the net contributors. The remaining 17 EU countries receive more than they pay in.

I can't help but somehow false incentives are being given here too.

The Brexit has left the EU with two further problems: firstly, the EU is losing the second largest net contributor and, with the loss of the British, the southern states, those who are not doing so well, now have the majority of votes in the EU Parliament. It will certainly be exciting to see what this means in reality.

Summary Euro

From a fiscal policy point of view, the EU is a single disaster because the ECB is unable to provide the individual member states with the necessary measures. This creates a Community liability that must be borne by all and ultimately by the taxpayer. In the coming weeks and months we will see what the impact will be when the full extent of the financial losses caused by Covid-19 comes to light.

The euro has compounded all the disadvantages of a fiat currency with the impossibility of satisfying all EU countries.

Cash abolition

In the previous chapters I have tried to explain the FIAT system and show some shortcomings. For some time now the abolition of cash has been under discussion, a prankster who thinks evil.

If we briefly recall the danger of a bank run (customers of commercial banks want to withdraw their deposits), the abolition of cash takes on a whole new quality. Cashless payments can almost completely prevent such bank runs, as it is now only possible to pay by card or smartphone.

This in turn requires an account with a bank or payment service provider who provides a card or smartphone app. By paying without cash we are finally driven into a dependence with the banks. In a cashless system it makes little sense to keep cash under the pillow, as it cannot be used in an emergency.

To be on the safe side, some EU countries have already introduced ceilings for cash payments, and the EU is discussing whether to introduce a European scheme.

In Germany, there is no upper limit yet, but for payments over 10,000 euros the data must be recorded, so it is no longer an anonymous transaction.

In 2020, the limit for anonymous purchases of precious metals will be lowered from 10,000 euros to 2,000 euros for the so-called over-the-counter transactions. This is to prevent the flight into precious metals and thus the state's withdrawal of control.

Under the guise of the fight against money laundering and terrorist financing, all these restrictions are introduced and, surprisingly, meet with little resistance from the public.

It is also often argued that cash is too expensive. It has to be transported, stored, produced/printed and it is simply no longer up to date. Since Covid-19, it is also much too dirty and can transmit diseases, so it is also dangerous.

In the next chapter I will look in more detail at the consequences of these measures.

The consequences

What bothers me most about these measures is that the entire population is placed under general suspicion. Basically, governments assume that we are all criminals. It is up to each individual to decide to what extent this is true.

The next worrying consequence is total surveillance. In a cashless society, the elites know when, who, where and what they have bought. It is obvious whether the person in question is often abroad or only travels in his or her immediate vicinity. In short, the transparent citizen has come into being.

Very often the argument comes from the population that they have nothing to hide. This statement is one of the stupidest a person can make. This implies that anyone can go home to these people at any time and look in their bedroom cupboard to see what their wife is wearing in her underwear or if there are any adult toys lying around. Of course you should also be allowed to look at the accounts and bank statements because you have nothing to hide. The fact is that in a cashless society, this is exactly what happens, except that you don't know who is looking in your cupboard. It is obvious where and what the wife buys in underwear, in which erotic shop, what was bought, etc.

It's not about whether I have something to hide, it's about deciding what I want to reveal and what I don't want to reveal. In most countries this is done under the protection of privacy, which is enshrined in the constitution.

So, if you ever hear someone say "I have nothing to hide". Why don't you just pay that person a visit.......

As already mentioned, these measures force us into the arms of the banks and thus bind us to the fiat monetary system. We are helplessly at the mercy of fee increases and other restrictions imposed by banks and governments. In addition to the complete screening of citizens, a cashless system also allows some dangers for the monetary system and the banks to be circumvented (e.g. a bank run).

As far as the price of cash is concerned, i.e. transport, storage and production costs, it is surprising that this was not a problem until a few years ago. Suddenly, these costs are barely bearable and are piling up the banks' balance sheets?

Another important issue is legislation. The euro is official currency and must be accepted to settle debts. Which means nothing other than that I can pay at any time with a euro banknote or euro coins (max 50) and the notes and coins must be accepted.

Last but not least, there is the question of how the whole thing should work in case of a power failure. Weather extremes have increased in recent years, floods and mudflows are becoming more frequent and with them the number of regional and national power cuts. Pipelines are being torn down or entire towns are under water, in such cases a purely cashless society would be an absolute disaster.

We will see what the future brings, but I hope I have given some of the "I have nothing to hide" citizens food for thought.

CBDC/ Central Bank Digital Currency
Digital Central Bank Currency

Anyone who now believes that the gradual abolition of cash is already everything is unfortunately sorely mistaken. The next step is the digital central bank currencies.

Future dreams, by no means. Central banks around the world are tinkering with digital currencies, and China is likely to lead the way.

"As long as I control the currency, I don't care who makes the laws!"
Baron Amschel Mayer Rothschild

But what are the CBCDs really about? As we know, the central bank issues the cash and lends euros, dollars, etc. to the banks. The banks, in turn, issue loans and create book or fiat money when lending. Around 90% of currencies are available purely electronically, in the form of numbers in bank accounts. Only about 10% are cash and thus issued by central banks.

Central banks therefore need commercial banks to manage the supply of money. High key interest rates to bring fewer euros into circulation, because this will increase the interest rates on bank loans. Low-key interest rates to put more euros into circulation because the loans become cheaper.

By going through the commercial banks, it is possible that not exactly what the central banks would like to see happens.

Especially now in the Corona crisis, this bottleneck is becoming apparent at the commercial banks. The states guarantee emergency loans for companies and private individuals.

The commercial banks should issue the emergency loans to companies and private individuals as quickly as possible. Only this is not done or only very slowly.

If all businesses and individuals had accounts with the central bank, the central bank would be able to transfer the credit amounts to the respective central bank account of the businesses and individuals much faster. This system would bypass the commercial banks and give the central banks a monopoly on currency creation.

In Switzerland, the "Full Money Initiative" was voted on in 2018 and rejected by around 75% of the population. The aim of the full-money initiative was that every franc should come from the central bank and the commercial banks should lose the right to create currency.

At first glance, this looks like a great idea. The population no longer has to worry about their deposits because now the central bank keeps the hard-earned salary and can always print enough currency in case things get tight.

During crisis, every citizen gets emergency aid credited to the central bank account without having to make tedious applications to the commercial banks. All in all a great thing.

But let us now look at the other side of the coin.

In the present system there is no monopoly on currency creation. Central banks buy all kinds of debt in times of crisis. Government bonds, corporate bonds and even stocks to support the states and the economy. In quiet times, central banks buy government bonds, but not necessarily directly from governments, but from the institutions that buy government bonds at auction. The central banks are, more or less, still independent of the states.

The second pillar of currency creation lies with the commercial banks, which put currency into circulation in the form of loans.

With CBDCs, the fundamental change is fundamental. The central banks now have a monopoly on currency creation. Remember the quote from Baron Amschel Mayer Rothschild, shouldn't that give us pause for thought?

The next thing that will happen is that taxes, fines and other charges can be debited directly from citizens' accounts. As cash is already being abolished, citizens will no longer be able to escape total control. Thinking further ahead, these central bank accounts can also be used to easily implement other restrictions.

As is already commonplace in China, for example, travel restrictions and other sanctions can be easily implemented. You have been speeding and flashing twice a month, and next month your fuel supply will be limited to 50 litres.

You were seen at a demonstration against the latest government laws, in future you will not be able to buy a metro ticket.

Utopia? On the contrary, this system is already in use in China. Face recognition, shopping behaviour, etc. Everything is monitored and if you misbehave, from the point of view of the state, you will be sanctioned.

But where do these CBDCs suddenly come from? Until a few months ago, they were not even known about and were at best discussed by the elites in back rooms.

The trigger was LIBRA. LIBRA is a cryptocurrency that Mark Zuckerberg from Facebook wanted to bring to the market. Via Facebook LIBRA would have over 2 billion users immediately. The idea is to send LIBRA and thus currencies via Facebook account.

You will now ask yourself what is new about it, something similar has been done by Bitcoin for almost 11 years. That's absolutely right, but the volume of Bitcoin is still tiny and its use for payment is still far from universal. So the classic cryptocurrencies do not yet pose a major threat to the powerful.

But LIBRA would have over 2 billion potential users worldwide from the first minute. LIBRA does not need central banks or commercial banks, just like all other cryptocurrencies. But LIBRA is many times larger than the entire crypto currency market. Therefore, LIBRA represents a huge danger for the power of the elites and is fought on all fronts.

I personally think little of LIBRA as it is linked to a Fiat currency basket and Facebook is not known for its careful handling of user data.

But LIBRA has managed in a very short time to make the elites' bottoms go down, I find that amusing.

For this reason, almost all central banks are working frantically on CBDCs.

Again for your understanding, CBDCs are not cryptocurrencies! CBDCs are electronic fiat currencies, similar to the book or fiat money of commercial banks. The only difference is that through CBDCs the central banks take over the currency monopoly and thereby generate a considerable gain in power.

Summary Fiat currencies

In the second part, I have tried to explain the basic functions in our fiat monetary system. It should have become clear that every euro, Swiss franc, dollar etc. is based solely on debt. The whole system is very similar to a snowball system, which can only be kept alive by new debts.

It should also have become clear that in a Fiat system it is not the general masses who benefit, but only very few at the top.

The creeping ban on cash will make us all transparent, and we will become more and more dependent on the goodwill of banks and governments. We are becoming system lemmings and George Orwell's novel is being put into practice. The CBDCs are another step towards Orwell.

Covid-19

As I mentioned at the beginning of the book, most of this book was written during the Covid-19 crisis.

We now know what money must be able to do and that the euro is not money but a currency. We now also know how a fiat currency system works and where the weaknesses lie. With all this knowledge we now look at what happens during the Corona crisis:

We all know that the crisis has virtually shut down the whole world. This means that the production and supply of services has been greatly reduced. Meanwhile, estimates suggest that the economy has contracted by around 5%.

When we recall how prosperity is created and how inflation depends on economic growth, all the alarm bells should now start ringing loudly.

We know that currency devaluation occurs when the volume of currency grows faster than economic output. We have just learned that economic output will collapse by around 5%.

This means that the ratio of currency volume to economic output has changed and that the contraction of the economy is causing an inflation of the currency volume and hence its devaluation. To keep prices "stable", currency would now have to be withdrawn from circulation.

But the opposite is happening, on an unprecedented scale. The central banks have opened all the floodgates and are flooding the countries with currency.

All countries are handing out billions in emergency aid, guaranteeing loans to support businesses and in the United States cheques are being handed out to all citizens to cover the most necessary expenses.

Here, two problems arise together, and these two problems multiply each other. Firstly, the economy is going down on its knees because less can be produced and secondly, the countries are being flooded with currency. To make matters worse, less is being spent because half the world is at home.

This scenario may work halfway through for a few more months, but by the time the pandemic is over, at the latest, we will be plunged straight into a global economic crisis.

Against what is rolling towards us, the crisis of 2008 is a child's birthday, a mild breeze.

Please do not misunderstand me, of course we must do everything we can to help our fellow human beings, there is no question about that.

However, it is clear that in recent years not everything has been as rosy as we were always led to believe. The economy is strong as never before, our companies are doing brilliantly, and so on.

This raises the question of why our oh-so-strong companies do not survive even two months without needing state-guaranteed aid loans.

For the one-person companies and the small and medium-sized enterprises, the situation is in most cases even bleaker. And once again it is the poorest who are hit hardest.

The whole, debt-based system, the years of 0% interest rate environment and the waste of taxpayers' money (Hello Mr. Scheuer, and many more) made it almost impossible to generate reserves and tempted the companies to accumulate debts, which in a normal interest rate environment would mean immediate insolvency.

(Andreas Scheuer is Minister of Transport in Germany. He wanted to introduce a toll system on German motorways, but failed due to an EU court ruling. As a result, Mr Scheuer has squandered some €530 million. This is the amount to be paid to the contracted companies as an advance payment)

All these grievances are now to be remedied with many more euros. Once again attempts are being made to put out fires with petrol and yes, this time it will not work either.

In the next two short chapters I would like to look at the situation in a gold standard.

In gold standard

In this and the next chapter, I will briefly discuss what would be different in a gold standard and how this difference could affect it. Let's start with the credits.
One main difference is that the money lent was earned by the lender. Be it through renunciation, saving or acting wisely. In the broadest sense, the available money represents a surplus which is not immediately needed and can therefore be lent.
Another phenomenon would also occur immediately, namely much higher interest rates.
Everyone can ask himself how much interest he would charge if he lent 1000 euros of his saved money for one year.

I am sure the percentage would be somewhere between 10 and 15 percent. Against this simple background, the current minus interest rates also appear in a completely different light.

Now let's look at what else would happen in terms of credit in a gold standard:
There would be much less credit, firstly because there would be fewer surpluses, and secondly because interest rates would be much higher, so that many people would not be able to afford credit. Another consequence would be that the borrower would have to offer much more collateral to obtain a loan at all. This would mean that not everything could be bought on credit and the per capita debt of the population would fall dramatically.
At first sight it looks like a step back into the Stone Age but only at first sight. More on this in the next chapter, where we will look at the bigger picture.

Gold Standard vs. Fiat

As we saw in the last chapter, there would be some changes at the credit level and it may seem that a gold standard is tantamount to a step backwards.
In this chapter, let us take a look at whether it would really be a step backwards.
Let us start at the beginning, with the currencies. Since money cannot simply be invented out of thin air in a gold standard, inflation is a much smaller problem, at least not if gold coverage is 100%. Of course, gold is also subject to fluctuations. Only these fluctuations are caused by the market and are therefore based on supply and demand, not on artificial reproduction by central and commercial banks. This will also translate into truly stable prices, as purchasing power will not steadily decline.

Under such circumstances, money could again act as a store of our work, since inflation, as already mentioned, would be much lower or even complete. This would stop the expropriation of the poorer sections of the population and the situation would slowly but steadily improve.

Also saving again makes sense, firstly you get reasonable interest on your savings and secondly the savings are not eaten up by inflation. Therefore, less credits would be needed because you can save the money yourself.

On the other hand, crafts would probably experience a new boom. It can be assumed that the currently predominant disposable mentality would soon be put to one side and a higher standard of quality would automatically take hold.

I assume that it will no longer be financially viable, for example, to buy T-shirts for 5.- euros, which are thrown away after being worn twice because they have lost their shape or dissolve into their components after the first wash.

I believe that the trend will be towards more expensive but higher quality T-shirts. These T-shirts would survive several washes and could be worn for longer. The cost per wear (purchase price : number of wear) would be significantly reduced.

I can also imagine that defective items would be repaired rather than thrown away. For everyday items, the price per use would go down significantly. I leave fashionable influences and must-haves out.

This should have the consequence that producers of cheap goods would have to say goodbye to the market or even change their production.

Other effects?

For example, since banks would have to lend their own money, they would probably look very closely at who was getting a loan. The problem that triggered the last crisis, subprime loans (loans to uncreditworthy customers) would also have been solved immediately.

In this context, the speculative behaviour on the stock exchanges would also change considerably because suddenly one's own money would be at stake.

It is also quite realistic that, for the reasons mentioned above, some laws regulating banks could be dropped.

Furthermore, state bank bail-outs and other rescue schemes would no longer be affordable because the necessary reserves would simply not be available and thus the wrong incentive for the banks would be gone because if the bank gambles away its own capital is at stake and not the taxpayer.

The conclusion is that states, banks and companies that do not act economically or take high risks will become insolvent and, in the case of banks and companies, disappear from the market.

Without going into further detail, it should have become clear that a gold standard would have eliminated key risks that had triggered the recent crises.

In the third part of the book, I go into more detail about the advantages of a covered currency, but there covered by a cryptocurrency.

But it should also be clear that a gold standard would require a complete rethink in society, because a stinginess is cool - or throw-away mentality would no longer work. But that is where I see the biggest problems.

A social problem

The population, especially the younger ones, was trimmed for consumption throughout their lives. I always wonder how it is possible that hardly 20-year-olds can drive cars for 50,000 and more.

Please don't misunderstand me, I have nothing against young people or expensive cars and if I had had the opportunity back then, I would certainly have taken it.

That the majority of these cars are financed should be clear, that a young person with, at best, a journeyman's examination can afford a 60.000.- Euro car after 3 years of work experience, I seriously doubt. If I only look at the maintenance costs of my modest everyday car (Renault Clio year 2011) and it is paid for, the calculation cannot work out.

An example, representative of the thinking of today's youth, was given to me by a former, young colleague.

He and his siblings received, for whatever reason, 30,000 euros in start-up capital. My colleague used it to finance a BMW M6 for a good 100,000 Euros. He used the 30,000. - as his own contribution for a 5-year leasing contract. The monthly instalment due was around 900.- and the buy-back value was around 30.000.-. The car thus cost 60x 900.- = 54,000.- plus the down payment of 30,000. -, i.e. around 84,000.-. However, since the car was a leased car, even after paying 84,000. - in five years, the car still did not belong to my colleague, since a residual value of about 30,000. - was still open. So if he bought the car, provided he could get the 30,000. - together, the car cost him 114,000.-.

Currently, 5-year-old M6s are traded for 50 – 60.000.-, depending on the mileage. If he can sell the car, let's say for 60,000. - the car has cost him 54,000. - in 5 years, that is over 10,000. - per year, and he has exactly nothing left of that. Neither the car nor the original 30.000.-.

If he can't raise the 30.000.-, he will have destroyed 84.000.-, BMW driving, in 5 years. The annual maintenance costs of around 2000 (fully comprehensive insurance, service, fuel, etc.) are not even taken into account. (The figures are only approximate and are for illustrative purposes).

But the frightening thing about this example is the statement of the former colleague: That's quite normal, everyone does that, and he would do the same again any time.
It is precisely this way of thinking that our elites want. In this way, the population is tied to the banking system without any real prospect of ever being self-sufficient and independent. They have to put up with all the L.F.Is (Lagarde's funny ideas) and have almost no chance to break out of the vicious circle.

(*Christine Lagarde is the new President of the ECB. She was convicted in France by a court of law:" of having been negligent in the handling of state funds and having allowed the misappropriation of state funds.* ")

As long as the fiat currency system works, at least on the outside, young adults will have no reason to change their lifestyle, which is why you can be ultra-cool on credit and use, not own, things that you can't even come close to affording. Only what happens when the system becomes unstable, which it already is, and the economy starts to weaken. How does my example colleague want to free himself from the debt trap when he is unemployed?
Another effect of this educated way of thinking is no less worrying. As soon as something does not go according to plan, the state is immediately called in. New laws, prohibitions and regulations are needed, negating the fact that the state that is called upon to help is responsible for all the evil. So one voluntarily turns the buck into a gardener and wonders why things are getting worse instead of better.

Frighteningly, this attitude, if thought through to its logical conclusion, leads to a totalitarian

State in which everything and everyone is dependent on the state and everything and everyone is controlled by the state. I am quite sure that if you ask around in society, nobody wants such a totalitarian scenario, but that is exactly where this prevailing attitude leads.

Search for causes:

The question now is of course how it could have come to this. It is important for me to make it clear that this chapter is not intended to be an attack on generations and their actions. Each of us is a child of his time and tries to get along in this time, some successfully and some less. But criticism of the behaviour of that time must be allowed.

If we look at the people after the Second World War, these people who were faced with nothing have started to rebuild their cities, villages and countries. With the scarce resources available and to the best of their knowledge.

At the end of the 1960s, people took to the streets and fought for peace, equality and social justice, even to the best of their ability.

Today, students take to the streets to demonstrate against environmental pollution and the inaction of the elites in environmental protection, even to the best of their ability.

Unfortunately, we still see the effects of the 68 movement today.

The anti-authoritarian upbringing of the 1970s and 1980s certainly had its good points, but it also almost completely prevented a healthy degree of personal responsibility and dealing with the unpleasant consequences of actions.

Of course, it is nice when I can do what I want as a child and not have to expect sanctions.

The only problem is that the real world works differently and these children have not been and are not even remotely prepared for the real world. Numerous egoists and sometimes unscrupulous fellow human beings have also emerged from this.

We are seeing the consequences of this today. Hardly anyone with the backbone to stand up and admit a mistake. It is always the others who are to blame. Personal responsibility and respect for other people and their property are almost non-existent. This begins in kindergarten and ends with our elites, whereby the elites fight for their power and have a different motivation.

As an example I would like to cite a situation I have experienced myself:

I had a job in a hotel near a school. We were waiting for the arrival of our truck, which should arrive in a few minutes. We were standing at the entrance to the loading lift, where there is a sign with an absolute stopping ban to ensure the loading and unloading of the trucks at all times.

Suddenly, a large volume car shot up and stopped right in front of the access road. When the driver got out and wanted to take her daughter by the hand, we asked her to move her car, as it was in the way of our truck and in the no stopping zone. Meanwhile the truck came and blocked the whole road. What followed was a tirade from the mother's mouth and the remark that it was our fault if her daughter was late for school. No sooner said than done, she got back in the car and roared away.

Two things have given us serious thought.

Firstly, the daughter would simply have had to get out of the car to walk the 150 metres or so to school alone. The daughter was an estimated 12 years old. The route would have taken her through a little-used side street and over a main road secured by traffic lights. But this was obviously much too dangerous for the poor child.

Secondly, passing on to us the mother's inability to leave home in time.

Now, if I may ask, how is the girl ever going to cope with any problems when Mrs. Mama is not around, who would probably not be much help either.

Unfortunately, these are the consequences which, in my opinion, go back to the 68ers. Of course, one must not lump everything and everyone together, but the tendency is unfortunately more than visible.

So how are the problems to be solved in the future when a generation appears on the scene that has neither respect for its fellow human beings and their property nor a backbone to face any problems.

The students of Fridays for Future have a similar problem. It speaks in their favour that they take to the streets, demonstrate for environmental protection and, at least superficially, bring about a change of mood. But it is of very little use if a Greta Thunberg speaks or rather shouts in front of the UN. First, the very people who created the problems are sitting there and have no interest in changing anything, and second, it is always a bad idea to insult people when you want something from them. It is also not very helpful to constantly insult the older generations by saying that they are to blame for everything.

This is not about the need for change, it is about how Mrs Thunberg and her supporters act.

Here, too, all generations have acted in good conscience and within their means. The fact that it was not always ideal is beyond question and may need to be adapted.

But in this case, too, everything is again being blamed on the others and rights are being claimed that only exist because the older generations have fought for them.

Again, climate change is real and it threatens the population in the future. Better yesterday than today, measures must be taken to mitigate the consequences.

But it must also be clear that such a revolution must take place from the bottom up.

A state does not help at all, states are always reacting and never acting. However, since a revolution can take place from the bottom up, the tone must change fundamentally. Accusations and insults will not help, and there will never be any cooperation in this way, especially when joint action is essential.

To make a difference, an approach has proved to be quite useful in the past. **DON'T TALK, SHOW.** It would already be a start if the ladies and gentlemen students were not driven to school in their cars, if the smartphone was not replaced by a new one every year and if cheap clothes were not constantly bought just because they were IN.

But to act in this way, a certain amount of self-confidence is needed and personal responsibility is needed, and that is exactly what will be difficult.

I would like to make it clear that the behaviour I have described does not apply to everyone, of course. In my circle of acquaintances there are some families who not only talk, but also do. Unfortunately, these families are still in the minority, I hope that this will change in the future.

In the third part of the book I try to develop a system covered by cryptocurrencies.

Part 3:

Introduction

I would like the third part of this book to lead to a lively discussion.

These only present my own view of things here. I am well aware that there are countless views, which are of course just as valid. Furthermore, in the third part, I will try to present my explanations as simply and easily understandable as possible. As already mentioned at the beginning of the book, I would like to reach laymen and people with no previous knowledge to show them what all goes wrong and what a possible solution might look like.

I will use Bitcoin as a proxy in the third part. I am aware that the properties of Bitcoin are only of limited use for a "world currency" but most people have at least heard of Bitcoin and associate it with crypto-currencies.

Why not gold?

I am absolutely certain that gold will retain its value even in a crypto-based monetary system. As already described at the beginning of this book, gold and silver have proven themselves as money for several thousand years and are accepted almost worldwide.

However, I am seriously concerned about the enormous environmental damage caused by the mining operations, some of which are illegal. If the world were to revert to a gold standard today, I believe that this environmental destruction would take on far more dramatic proportions, destroying vast areas of nature forever.

On the other hand, in the future it will be possible to trace the origin of the gold very closely. The use of such a system would probably reduce the number of illegal mines and thus relieve the burden on nature. Thus, the problem would be reduced, but until that happens I would refrain from a gold standard.

The situation today

Before I go into the third part, it seems important to me to say a few words about the SWIFT system and the US dollar.

The SWIFT system (Society for Worldwide Interbank Financial Telecommunication) is a messaging system used to process international payments. In a way, the system is by the banks for the banks. SWIFT has its headquarters in Belgium and is therefore subject to European law. Thanks to the SWIFT system it is possible to exclude whole countries from international trade by blocking access to the system (Iran 2012). Within a very short period of time Iran experienced a downturn in foreign trade and the Iranian economy came into severe distress.

Originally designed to facilitate trade between countries, the system was used as a weapon against a state. I am in no way prejudging this measure, I am simply showing that it is possible. We see that this system can put whole countries in trouble if they do not dance to the tune of influential elites.

The US dollar is the leading currency in global trade in goods. This means that a large proportion of goods are settled in US dollars (e.g. oil, gold, etc.), regardless of whether the United States is involved or not. For example, if Saudi Arabia sells oil to Germany, the oil is paid for in dollars.

There are some countries that are seeking to switch to other currencies, but these are not yet very far advanced.

The fact that the US dollar is used as a global trading currency entails some risks. The United States may appreciate or depreciate its currency at any time and thus manipulate prices on world markets.

In this short chapter I wanted to show briefly that there are at least two ways of manipulating world trade. Both means are controlled by Western states and can present the rest of the world with major challenges. Balance looks different somehow.

But now the blockchain technology continues.

Functionality of a blockchain

In this chapter I would like to explain the basic functioning of a blockchain. It does not deal with technical details, but only illuminates the function and the resulting innovations.

A blockchain is a network in which all participants have equal rights and absolute agreement (consensus) on the truth of the content.

To explain this in more detail, I will use the example of a cash book.

Every transaction, i.e. every transfer of Bitcoins from one person to another, is recorded in this cash book. Every 10 minutes these transactions are checked, confirmed and entered on a new page of the cash book. This new page is then sent to all participants in the network and attached to the back of the existing cash book. Thus, the same level of knowledge is maintained throughout the network. All this happens only through the network and the underlying mathematical and cryptographic rules. There is no need for a third instance to control and monitor these processes.

The network and the transactions it contains can be viewed by anyone at any time. There is absolute transparency. As this cash-book is stored on around 60,000 computers scattered around the world, the network is extremely secure and it is almost impossible to change stored data afterwards.

The question remains where the Bitcoins come from. The Bitcoins are created as a reward for the network participants (miners) who control and confirm the transactions and enter them on the new page. The maximum number of Bitcoins is mathematically limited to 21 million and the last one will be born around 2140. Around 18 million Bitcoins are currently in circulation (as of Nov. 19)

The following is a summary of the basic functions:

Absolute transparency
No external supervisory authority necessary
No subsequent change of data possible
Absolute consensus on the content
Maximum 21 million bitcoins in 2140

We have seen that artificial reproduction of Bitcoins is impossible. It is not possible simply to print a few million more, which in turn makes artificial inflation impossible.

We have also seen that the network cannot be manipulated by anyone and therefore no subsequent changes can be made to the data.

Furthermore, the network does not need any external control authority, since the entire network is based only on mathematical and cryptographic rules.

So much for the function and characteristics of a blockchain, now we dive into a possible financial system based on the Bitcoin.

Bitcoin instead of dollars

As already mentioned at the beginning of the third part, I use the Bitcoin as an avatar. From a technical point of view, the Bitcoin network is not suitable for a base currency, as the transaction rate is limited to about seven transactions per second. But since the Bitcoin is the oldest and therefore the best known cryptocurrency, I will use it as a proxy for simplicity. In a real environment a cryptocurrency based on a DAG (Directed Acyclic Graph) would solve the task almost perfectly.

So, what would happen now if we replaced the lead currency, the US dollar, with Bitcoin?

Firstly, the SWIFT system would no longer be needed with immediate effect and could therefore no longer be used for sanctions against individual states. Since the transactions in the Bitcoin network are peer-to-peer, i.e. directly from sender to recipient, a third instance such as SWIFT is unnecessary. Secondly, it is no longer possible for individual countries in the Bitcoin network to revalue or devalue a currency. This would mean that the United States would no longer be able to influence the world market.

Point of criticism

It is often argued that there is too little gold to cover a currency. This argument will certainly be applied to Bitcoin. In the following I will list some arguments which put this objection into perspective.

The Bitcoin has eight decimal places, the Satoshis, i.e. to a certain extent the Bitcoin cents. This means that each Bitcoin contains 100 million Satoshis. If you now add 100 million times the approximately 18 million Bitcoins, you get a considerable amount of currency units. Depending on the assigned value of a Satoshi, large amounts can be represented. In a newly developed DAG, the number of coins and the decimal places can be freely configured, so it would be possible to map the total stock of world debt and thus the worldwide stock of currencies.

That brings us to the next point.

It is also often overlooked that the actual number that adorns a coin or banknote, i.e. the face value, is completely irrelevant. The essential thing is the ratio.

As an example, we take an average flat. As a starting point, we assume that a flat costs 1/3 of a person's monthly income in rent. If this person earns 3000 euros, the flat will cost 1000 euros a month in rent. If the income is 3 euros and the flat costs 1 euro rent, the person's financial situation has not changed.

The same applies to the economy. Whether a product has a production cost of €1 and a selling price of €2, or whether the production cost is €1000 and the selling price is €2000, is completely irrelevant. For the producer, only the relationship between the production and sales price is relevant.

Of course, for a currency, the face value should be chosen so that the calculation is simple and not to use infinite digits before and after the decimal point, but these are purely practical considerations and have nothing to do with the quantity of the underlying value. (Gold or even Bitcoin).

National currencies

How would the individual national currencies behave in the case of a Bitcoinfixing? First of all, fixed exchange rates to other Bitcoin-covered currencies would immediately result. For example, as 4 francs Français used to correspond to one Swiss franc. It should not be forgotten that the national currencies and their denominations are nothing more than quantity specifications for Satoshis and Bitcoins. To return to the example of the franc, the French would have deposited one franc with a Satoshi and the Swiss one franc with 4 Satoshis, which would make the ratio 4:1 again. Again, it is clear that the face value of a banknote reflects nothing more than the assigned amount of Satoshis.

This leads us to the next question: "how should the face value be determined"?

Option 1

As a first step, the price of a bitcoin could be set at €10 million. This value would allow a Satoshi to represent the equivalent of 10 euro cents. Based on this price, one could now determine the average gross salary in the respective countries in Bitcoin and Satoshis. Since, as we have seen above, all prices are in proportion to each other, all prices, be they goods or services, should automatically result within a short time.

Again, to explain these circumstances. An average flat costs about 1/3 of an average monthly salary, a litre of milk costs about 1/1600 of an average monthly salary and a new middle-class car costs about 15 average monthly salaries. We see with this method one could realize a transition from a Fiat currency system, to a Bitcoin covered system. This method would also leave intact the different price levels in the various countries.

But that is only half the task. Since the currencies have to be backed by Bitcoin, the individual countries must of course have a certain number of Bitcoins. At first sight this seems logical, but there is also a danger. Since it is of course easier for rich nations to buy large quantities of Bitcoins, while poorer nations are not able to do so, a position of power of the industrial nations would establish itself initially, and that is exactly what must be prevented. The goal must be that all countries participating in Bitcoin coverage start from the same starting point. This is the only way to ensure that everyone has the same chances.

How could such a situation be achieved?

Scenario

One possible approach would be to take the population of the states as a basis, for example. Per 10,000 inhabitants 1 Bitcoin. This would give Germany with about 80 million inhabitants 8000 Bitcoins. These figures are only an example and depend on the maximum number of coins available.

If we were to take the number of inhabitants rather than the number of citizens as a basis, we would have triggered a small competition among the participating nations in advance. So each nation would consider how to attract as many people as possible. Be it through a low tax rate, excellent medical care or other incentives that make living in that nation seem desirable. Because the more inhabitants a nation has, the more Bitcoin it receives as starting capital.

If we think further ahead in such a scenario, we discover relatively quickly that low-wage countries can generate an advantage from this situation.

Take Germany, for example, with a gross monthly salary of around 3300 euros, and Iran with around 400 euros gross monthly salary.

Both countries have around 80 million inhabitants and can therefore be compared quite well.

If we now apply the previous approach, i.e. convert one Bitcoin per 10,000 inhabitants and the average gross content into Bitcoins, we can see that Iran would benefit considerably from this system. To illustrate this, the following small calculation example: In Germany the gross average salary is 3300 Euro, which corresponds to 33000 Satoshis. In Iran, the average income is €400, which corresponds to 4000 Satoshis. This means that the salary in Iran is still around 8 times lower than in Germany. However, since both countries have the same basic stock of Bitcoins, due to their population, Iran now has a considerable advantage.

Iran would now have several options. One of these would be to convert the entire Bitcoin stock into currency units and put them into circulation. This would have the consequence that wage and price levels would rapidly converge with those in Germany.

Another option would be to hoard the surplus Bitcoins and not to put more currency into circulation. This would allow Iran to inflate its own currency if necessary. But only as far as the Bitcoin stocks are sufficient. Iran would thus have more possibilities to control its currency.

Another option would be investment in infrastructure (in the best case) or upgrading the military Force (in the worst case). This would of course also lead to a certain inflation and would bring prices closer to those of the Germans, albeit via detours.

We could now change the assumptions and, for example, take GDP per capita (gross social product) as a starting point or use some other value. But we will never arrive at a reasonable solution. Especially since sometimes the poorer countries and sometimes the richer countries would be advantaged. On this basis, it is almost impossible for a consensus to be reached between the states.

Moreover, the liberal idea of Bitcoin is completely neglected. Who decides how the division is made? Who decides what the value of a Bitcoin is? These questions could be continued almost endlessly and would almost certainly not get anywhere, as Bitcoin does not need or allow outside interference.

Let us therefore move on to,

Option 2

This possibility takes a completely different approach and is already emerging in some countries. Gold and silver have been known as means of payment for about 6000 years and have prevailed over shells, gems, etc. Over the centuries, the free market has led to gold and silver being accepted as means of payment almost worldwide, even today. So gold and silver were not invented by states, but actually came from the population.

For a long time Argentina, Venezuela and a few other countries have been struggling with very high inflation (monetary devaluation). The national currencies are losing purchasing power almost daily, putting citizens in financial distress. As a reaction to this situation, citizens began to change their national currency into US dollars in order to avoid the fall in value of their own currency. Shortly afterwards, governments limited or even prohibited the purchase of foreign currencies.

In all these countries there is a steadily increasing demand for cryptocurrencies. The crisis-stricken population is increasingly trying to store their hard-earned money in crypto-currencies. Also, traders of food and goods of daily use increasingly accept cryptocurrencies as means of payment.

Of course, governments are trying to stop this behaviour, as it leads to a further weakening of the national currencies and thus undermines the control over the national currency and thereby the control over the population. So, it should be clear that governments are doing everything possible to prevent the spread of crypto-currencies.

We can see from these examples that the system changeover comes from the population. I believe that this is the only way to herald a system change. This can be achieved by creating more and more points of acceptance for crypto-currencies and by making the handling of the wallets (electronic purse) increasingly easier. More on this in the chapter on connection technologies.

Some may now argue that this is hardly possible and that governments will take drastic measures.

That may be true, but one must not forget that the state is actually there for the citizens and is maintained by them.

"If people are afraid of the state, we live in a tyranny; if the state is afraid of the people, we live in a liberal society. „

Source: Thomas Jefferson

That is exactly where we must go, to a liberal society.

There were and are enough examples of local currencies (Wörgl 1932, Schwanenkirchen 1930, etc.) that worked. As incredible as it sounds, there are still governments today that are not allowed to run up debts, the Isle of Sark is one such case. There is neither a state health insurance nor a state pension fund, but income tax and value added tax are foreign words.

If I want to have insurance, then I have to take care of it. Of course, this also requires a change in the population's thinking, but freedom also means work and personal responsibility.

In the next chapter I will show you a few small steps towards more independence and anonymity. All these steps are not meant to encourage you to commit crimes, they only show you how you can legally get back a little freedom. These possibilities are also not investment advice, I just want to show you what I do to regain a bit of independence. Of course, you have to decide for yourself what makes sense for you and what doesn't. Please check in your country if the measures are in accordance with the law before you start with a possible implementation.

Transformation from the population

The first thing we need to do is remember where the weaknesses lie in our current system. The state is trying to keep us under control through inflation. Since the whole system is based on debt, the aim is to give as many loans as possible to achieve further dependency of the population. Only the national currencies can be used to pay taxes and duties. Cash is to be phased out gradually.
This must suffice as a rough overview.

How do we get out of this mess now?

Let's just start withdrawing our money from the banks. Let's leave only as much money on the account as the monthly obligations can be paid, the rest we withdraw.
We can pay cash for everyday shopping, petrol, clothes, etc., at least for now. In this context it is also important to understand that the money on your account does not belong to you, it belongs to the bank! In return, the bank undertakes to pay back the amount in your account, but it does not say when or how. If things go badly, the bank can pay you 10 euros a week and you have little or no means of changing anything. (read the small print on your account)

What do we achieve through this?

Firstly, independence and anonymity. Secondly, we withdraw capital from the banks, which means they can issue fewer loans and generate less interest income. And, very importantly, the cash is ours again and no longer belongs to the bank.

Continue

In a further step we regularly buy cryptocurrencies. Bitcoin, Litecoin, Ethereum and Dash are accepted by almost all payment systems. We can do this via exchanges such as Bitpanda, Coinbase or, for example, Bison, or we use Bitcoin ATM's, so we would also be anonymous. Even with these crypto-currencies you can pay without any problems, provided the merchant accepts them. The number of acceptance points is constantly increasing, it will still take some time until
they are close to universal, but we are on the right track. More on this in the chapter "Connectivity technologies".

Those who cannot or do not want to do without plastic money should get a Visa card from e.g. WIREX, just to name one of several. The WIREX card can easily be loaded with Bitcoin, Litecoin, Dash, Ethereum and many other cryptocurrencies. If you want to use the card, simply change your cryptos to Euros, all in the app and in seconds and your Visa card is ready to use. As a bonus, there is a cash back in Bitcoin with every payment.

If you are in the lucky position and can build up monthly reserves, invest in physical gold, silver or other valuable assets.

If you still have debts on your credit card, pay them off. Your account balance is in minus, set it to zero, plus the amount needed for the monthly bills. Do not use any of your Payback and bonus cards any more. These programs are only aimed at your data and data is the gold of the 21st century. The problem is that not you benefit from your Data, it is the Cashback Issuer. If you are honest, you can easily do without the rewards and offers.

What have we achieved through these further actions?

We have taken another part of our assets out of the fiat currency system. By investing in precious metals or other assets such as watches, we protect ourselves against inflation and possible negative interest rates. We have also taken a further step towards anonymity and thus independence.

If you want to invest your money profitably, you have several possibilities to do so. All based on cryptocurrencies.

One option would be the Celsius Network. If you keep cryptocurrencies in your Celsius Wallet, you will be paid interest on them on a weekly basis.

Depending on the currency you hold, a little more or a little less but in any case considerably more than in your bank.

Maybe you would like to invest in real estate, no problem. REAL would be one option. Via REAL you can invest your crypto-currencies in real estate and receive monthly rental income or you can participate in the sale of the property. Always proportionate to your investment. These are only two of countless possibilities to invest your money and let it work for you.

Internet behaviour.

Parallel to the above steps, you are changing your internet behaviour. Reduce your online purchases to the bare essentials. Go to the clothes shop in your city and use the offers in your area. In this way you will help the local economy and Amazon will be able to cope if you generate less turnover there.

Change your browser, there's no reason for Google to turn your surfing habits into profits you don't get from. Use the Brave browser instead of Google Chrome. Brave rewards you for your attention while surfing in the form of BAT, which is a cryptocurrency, prevents tedious pop-ups and most importantly, Brave does not give out any data. The Google search engine can be replaced by DuckDuckGo or Frontpage, which do not track your search queries and habits.

If you use applications such as Google Docs and similar applications, stop using them. Hundreds of applications are on Blockstack that work at least as well but do not save your data. There is not a new login for every app where your data is requested. You log in everywhere with your decentralized identity from Blockstack. This identity belongs to you and the linked data is on the Blockchain in your own wallet. This data is only read out when you log in to an app, but is not stored anywhere.

These conversions give you a further degree of anonymity and thus escape the surveillance of internet giants and states.

Community and neighbourhood

I would now like to touch on what I consider to be a vital point. Take care of your neighbourhood, your family and your immediate surroundings. This also includes the local traders and shops. If the going gets tough, your internet acquaintance on the other side of the world is of no use to you at all. Then you need support from your immediate surroundings. This does not mean that you have to make inseparable friends with all your neighbours, it is enough to be friendly to them and exchange a word or two in the stairwell.

If we now look back and look at all these steps, we have already achieved a lot with relatively little effort. We have limited ourselves to what is absolutely necessary at the banks and thus escaped the negative interest rates and supervision.

We have taken some of our assets out of the Fiat system, protecting us from inflation and regaining some freedom and have created the possibility to do our daily shopping anonymously again, ergo even more freedom.

By shopping at local merchants, we support the local economy and thus deprive Internet merchants of our data and a small part of their power.

By reducing the number of online orders, we have also contributed to environmental protection, as fewer parcels have to be transported.

We no longer give away our data and therefore do not allow internet or supermarket groups to turn our data into profit. In addition, we are moving further in the direction of anonymity and thus personal freedom.

We maintain our direct relationships and are therefore not alone in an emergency.

If that looks like something, let's call it measly, to some people, I would ask you to multiply these measures by 100,000 people. The effect of these puny measures should be enormous.

Now we go one step further and start accepting payments in crypto-currencies as a private person. Let's say everything we need in the bank account to pay the monthly bills, plus the amount we need in cash for our daily purchases is paid in Euros, all the rest in Bitcoin.

You will ask yourself why my employer should do this? If the acceptance of crypto-currencies increases, it is easy for the employer to pay a part of the salaries in crypto-currencies. After all, he or she takes in crypto-currencies via his or her payment option.

If we, as a population, manage to establish parallel currencies in this way, then the state must once again be afraid of its citizens.

What comes next?

If we manage to put the above mentioned points into practice and also start to accept crypto-currencies as a means of payment for our own services, we can assume that the state will intervene.

These actions constitute a, more or less, direct attack on the monetary system and will not be accepted just like that. One of the first arguments will be that it jeopardizes financial stability and that we are endangering our economic system by such actions. Another argument that will be raised immediately is that money laundering and the financing of terrorism is an argument that can be used to justify just about any regulation or ban. This is absolutely right, at least in part, but it forces governments and central banks to act.

Depending on how the authorities act, i expect more rules and laws to be introduced, it becomes clear what governments are really after.

In this context, I would also like to mention that governments act in very few cases, governments are usually only ever reacting. This means that governments have to react retrospectively to circumstances that they cannot control, and thus almost always chase a trend or upheaval.

If governments now go in and make the handling of crypto-currencies and cash more difficult by laws and regulations, even the last citizen should slowly realize where the journey is to go.

One effect resulting from this finding could be a loss of confidence in the legal currency and thus a loss of confidence in the authorities and governments involved.

With this loss of confidence on the part of the population, alternative means of payment, those the population trusts, will slowly establish themselves (see Venezuela).

It is likely that this will not be a single global cryptocurrency, but rather that different currencies will establish themselves on different continents, territories or countries. In principle, these can also be state crypto-currencies, as long as they cannot be manipulated by states and are based on a decentralized, public network. It will depend on the population, which cryptocurrency will prevail and best meet their needs. It is very likely that some kind of cash will establish itself, covered by the respective crypto-currency. This may be due to technical obstacles, such as no internet or electricity, or for social reasons, for example, when people prefer to physically have notes and coins.

As a counter-argument, the impossibility of international payments could now be raised if a reserve currency such as the US dollar no longer existed. I will also deal with this issue in the chapter on follow-on technologies. Let me say in advance that it is absolutely no problem.

A look into the future

The introduction of crypto-currencies and the cash covered by crypto-currencies will also change a lot in the financial industry. I don't think banks will disappear, they will just have to go back to their original business model. The safekeeping of customers' money and the granting of loans. As already described in the chapter on the gold standard, interest rates will rise and banks will take a very close look at who is creditworthy and who is not, after all it is now a question of their own assets.

When a bank issues a loan, the bank must have the necessary capital and can no longer simply invent money out of thin air. This means that the bank has to generate profits and therefore reserves. In this way the banks participate in free competition. If the customers agree with the services and the prices, the bank will flourish, if not, the bank has to think of another strategy or it will disappear from the market.

Of course, a bank can also work with the client's money, if the client so wishes. This is also a classic business area for banks. They lend clients money and share the interest income with the clients. Trading in shares for customers should and must also take place to support the economy. To put it in a nutshell, the financial industry is doing again what it was originally intended for. It supplies companies with money and mediates between investors and companies. For private individuals, it ensures the safe storage of money and helps to finance larger purchases.

The bottom line is that the behaviour of all market participants will change, as it is now no longer possible to pay debts with new debts. Every market participant will have to change his business model in a way that he offers an interesting and good product for consumers to consume. If a market participant does not manage to do so, he will disappear from the market.

I see one of the most significant changes brought about by a pegged monetary system in the removal of false incentives by governments. During recent crises we have seen governments and central banks pumping vast sums of money into bailing out banks and other industries.

In doing so, they have shifted the economic responsibility of companies onto the citizen (bail out), who now has to use taxpayers' money to pay for the inability of company managers. In doing so, governments and central banks have created an environment in which there is no incentive for companies to operate economically and conscientiously. If anything goes wrong, the state, or more precisely the taxpayer, comes and rescues the companies. Through this environment, banks and companies have taken and are taking risks that they would never take if their own capital was at stake.

Such bail-outs are no longer possible in a covered monetary system, as these bail-outs would have to be paid for out of saved reserves and this will not happen. As I said, it is now one's own capital that is at risk, not money created from nothing.

The States

Let us now look at what this means for the state.

In a covered monetary system, governments and central banks, with central banks actually becoming unnecessary, can no longer simply create money out of nothing. This turns governments into, almost, ordinary market participants. Almost, because governments finance a large part of their expenditure through taxpayers' money, not through profits from a clever business idea. Since governments are now dependent on taxpayers, which they already are today, only they have probably forgotten it, they have to act from an economic point of view.

Tax promises made during an election campaign must now be paid for by the taxpayer's own resources, which will lead to a considerable decline in such promises.

Any kind of government expenditure would have to be analysed and calculated carefully because in the event of a miscalculation, the taxpayer's own assets, or in fact the taxpayer's assets, are at stake. Berlin Airport (BER), Stuttgart 21, Gorch Fock and many other government projects would not take place in this way and if they did, the people would call those responsible to account. In the current environment, incompetent ministers are being promoted to President of the EU without being held accountable for their actions.

(BER airport should have opened in June 2012. The current deadline is October 2020, and costs have almost tripled and currently stand at €7.1 billion. Stuttgart 21 is a railway station project which should have been opened in 2021. The new date is now 2025 and the current additional costs amount to 1.5 billion Euros. Gorch Fock is a sailing ship of the German Navy. The necessary repairs were calculated with 9.6 million Euro and should be finished after 17 weeks, that was 2015. The ship is still in the shipyard and the costs have risen to 135 million Euro)

There is absolutely no reason why states should not have their own businesses, be there health care facilities or infrastructure companies such as railways. However, these establishments must operate economically in a covered system and can no longer be supported by state subsidies. In such cases, it is up to the state to decide whether these companies must make a profit or only operate on a cost-covering basis.

Such a change would also encourage states to earmark their tax revenues for specific purposes. Personally, I have no problem with having to pay motorway tolls, but I have a big problem if these tolls are used to plug holes in the railways. (Please take this only as an example)

One possible approach could be a pay per use system, which means nothing other than that I pay for the service I actually use. With a cryptocurrency such models are quite feasible.

This would have a further influence on the behaviour of states. The state must now provide services and offers that represent added value for users and are therefore also used. If the offers are not used, states would either have to improve the offer or discontinue it, depending on its economic viability.

Because the states would suddenly have to work according to economic aspects, I assume that the state apparatus would shrink considerably and be limited to its actual tasks again. Infrastructure, internal and external security, health and possibly social tasks. This should also considerably reduce the tax burden on the working population and, as a nice side effect, there would probably be less undeclared work, since the craftsmen and services could now be afforded again.

Another important effect is likely to be in the form of reserves among the population. Many people move from one salary to the next and have no chance to build up reserves.

This is partly due to the exuberant tax and duty mania of the states and partly to inflation, which is constantly driving up prices.

With a covered monetary system and a lean state, these two unnecessary burdens would be corrected downwards and it would be possible to build up reserves again.

Fees and taxes

State social security schemes would also disappear in a further step. How is it possible that as a self-employed person in Austria I have to pay 27% social security? That means I have to work for about 3 months a year to pay an insurance that I do not need. In a stable currency system where my savings do not lose purchasing power every year, I can just as well save up my pension myself and do not have to use my contributions to plug the holes in other social insurance schemes. There is nothing to be said against the state offering a social insurance and if the state social insurance issues an attractive product, you can use it, voluntarily and not because I have to. I can easily insure visits to the doctor or possible hospital stays privately, at fixed monthly rates and not depending on income.

Another 3 months per year an average self-employed person in Austria works for taxes. In words: "Three months!"

$$0 – 11´000.- = 0 \%,$$
$$11 – 18´000.- = 25 \%,$$
$$18 – 31´000.- = 35\%,$$
$$31 – 60´000.- = 42 \%,$$
$$60 – 90´000.- = 48\%,$$
$$90 – 1´000´000.- = 50\%,$$
$$> 1'000'000.- = 55\%$$
(as of 10. 19)

Of course, these burdens do not only affect the self-employed, they affect everyone. Once again, it is clear that the incentives are completely wrong.

The more you try and try hard, the higher the penalty. A tax system that is independent of income and does not increase progressively would make much more sense. Let us take the classic "tithe" that was collected as tax in the past.

This means that although the amount of tax increases when I make an effort and therefore earn more, at the same time I have more left and the incentive is back on the right side. But if I constantly have to be careful not to move up to a higher tax bracket, the incentive is to do less and thus earn less, i.e. on the wrong side.

Another tax which mainly affects the poorer sections of the population are VAT.

In Austria, it is 20%. This tax is probably one of the most unfair of all. On the one hand, VAT is once again levied on salaries which have already been taxed and, on the other, it is once again the poorer people who are hit hardest.

The abolition of VAT would bring immediate and tangible relief to the poorer sections of the population. The counter-argument is certainly the welfare state. Only by levying these taxes it is possible to support the socially weaker. The question that arises is whether it would not make much more sense not to burden the socially weaker sections of the population in the first place, in which case aid for the socially weaker sections could be reduced or even abolished altogether.

In a state where the people are once again in charge, this frenzy of taxes and duties would probably disappear rapidly. If one now imagines a lean and efficient state, forced by a covered monetary system, the world looks much better.

I can already hear the cries of those people who see this system as a complete disregard for the most vulnerable sections of society. Rest assured, I have not forgotten them, the socially weaker ones.

If we look at the current system, we know that in future fewer and fewer working people will have to pay for more and more pensioners, which will not work in any way. But this trend is not new, it has been known for decades that sooner or later we will reach the limits of this system. Little or nothing has happened to address the problem.

Let's look at where the problems come from.

One of the biggest problems lies once again in our monetary system. Money <u>must</u> serve as a store of value. It is unacceptable that a currency, for example the euro, should lose more than 30% of its purchasing power since its introduction. These are the official figures, but in reality it should be much more.

We are in a situation where fewer and fewer young people have to pay for more and more older people and at the same time the currency is losing purchasing power every year due to inflation. This is a combination of two circumstances which have a negative impact on each other.

In a covered currency, at least the problem of inflation would be reduced and the savings of 20 years ago would retain their purchasing power, which in itself would significantly reduce the problem.

There is, in my view, nothing to be said against a fixed percentage of social security contributions; as long as these contributions are used for a specific purpose, I see no problem. But in my opinion, it must be a fixed percentage that applies to everyone.

This will, of course, put some people back on the barricades who want a higher percentage of the wealthy.

The question is why?

There will always be more hard-working, smarter or birth-preferred people, just as there will always be less hard-working, less smart and birth-preferred people.

Nothing in the world can change that.

Even if socialism is now probably being put back into the race, under socialism it was not equally good for everyone, but equally bad for everyone, except the elites, of course.

It does not make sense to punish people who have done more by increasing the percentage of taxes. This is tantamount to penalizing their efforts and again creates false incentives.

Why should someone make an effort, go to school longer, work more hours a day, take responsibility, take risks, if in the end he is punished for his efforts and dedication?

It makes no sense.

But to get back to the issue of the socially weaker ones.

When I hear that welfare recipients do not go to work because they are paid more by welfare than when they went to work, it makes me very thoughtful. I don't want to put the blame on these people, they just take advantage of the opportunities, which is very clever.

Here too, we see completely misguided incentives on the part of governments. Such incentives are no longer possible in a covered monetary system because the money needed for them is lacking.

It is not about forcing people to work, that should be decided by each person for himself, but he must also bear the consequences of his decision.

As already mentioned, freedom does not come for free, it requires a certain commitment and a high degree of personal responsibility.

Let's go back to the subject of pensioners, who are becoming more and more numerous and the younger people, who are becoming fewer and fewer.

In a monetary system which has not built in a loss of purchasing power every year while offering reasonable interest rates (see chapter on the gold standard), a significant contribution can be made to solving this problem.

On the one hand, the purchasing power of savings is maintained, savings generate interest income and, since purchasing power is maintained, the prices of goods and services do not rise but tend to fall. (More on this in the following chapter)

With the above-mentioned changes in purchasing power and interest rates, it should now also be possible to restructure the entire pension system.

It makes little sense if fewer and fewer people have to pay for more and more pensioners. If everyone saved for themselves, and this would be possible now, the age pyramid would no longer be of any consequence. This change could relieve the burden on young, working people, as they would be saving for themselves rather than having to support an ever-increasing number of pensioners.

It should also be clear that such a change of system cannot take place overnight, otherwise today's pensioners would suffer greatly. There are certainly ways of integrating a change of system smoothly, but this can only work with a lean state and a stable currency.

Why are the prices falling?

If we assume a constant purchasing power of money and assume that the economy produces further innovations in production and products, we can assume that more efficient and therefore profitable production improvements lead to lower prices. A manufacturer is only interested in the relationship between effort and profit. If he can produce more or better with less effort, he can reduce the sales price without losing profit and thus gain a competitive advantage.

For the above-mentioned reasons, it should be possible to finance a social system for those really affected and to substantially alleviate the demographic problem of fewer and fewer young people having to pay for more and more older people.

Environmental protection

A pegged monetary system, with associated interest rate rises and little or no loss of purchasing power, should also bring about some changes in the transport sector.

If they are honest, it is completely absurd to fly to London and back for 50 euros. This is only possible because airlines can refinance themselves through new debts and survive through all kinds of accounting tricks. It should be clear to everyone that with such low prices you can never cover your expenses. On-board personnel such as flight attendants, pilots or fuel, airport fees, maintenance costs and capital costs (financing) for the aircraft, all this cannot be covered by 25 euros per direction. In a covered currency system, the interest rates for financing the aircraft would also rise, which simply makes such low prices impossible.

A covered currency system also forces airlines to adopt a pricing model that at least covers costs, which is likely to increase air fares.

This would probably result in a reduction in the number of passengers and therefore less air traffic.

However, as people have more money at their disposal, summer holidays in Egypt, Turkey etc. should still be secure.

Since many meetings can now be held virtually and companies will look a little more closely at their expenses, I expect business trips to decrease.

However, some airlines are also likely to exit the market. As already mentioned, maintaining operations on credit will no longer work.

Rising air fares may also make it harder for exotic fruits, such as mangoes, to compete in the European market, as they would simply be much more expensive.

This could lead to a reduction in the areas under cultivation in the countries of origin and thus benefit the climate.

This effect is likely to affect other industries and cheaply curb imports from low-wage countries, as transport costs will rise.

I would like to make it clear that I am absolutely not an opponent of globalization.

Due to the tax and duty mania of the industrial nations, production was moved to low-wage countries. When Europe is no longer able to produce economically due to the tax and duty burden, the production facilities are moved to Asia and Latin America.

This problem has been aggravated by the stingy is horny mentality. During the Corona crisis, people were shocked to discover that there were no protective masks in Europe and that whole supply chains collapsed... how could this happen?

Concurrently, Western companies show little interest in the working and environmental conditions in low-wage countries, which has led to an increase in environmental pollution and working conditions.
We see here several circumstances which are intensified into the negative.

Financial Markets

I see a major problem with the financial markets in their present form. Apart from the financial transactions carried out on credit and with the taxpayer's guarantees, which would change immediately if the currencies were covered.
I find it ethically highly questionable that food speculation is possible. This is done, among other things, through futures betting on future crop yields. In its original form, these futures made sense because they guaranteed farmers and food suppliers a fixed price for their harvests. This allowed the producers to calculate in advance and gave them a certain amount of security in their actions. In a covered currency system, I still think this makes sense. But the problem today is that people speculate on the harvests with a lot of borrowed money and thus the natural price formation is completely taken to the point of absurdity.
Through short positions, which is a bet on falling prices, and all sorts of other instruments, the original idea of financial protection for manufacturers was turned into the opposite. In this way, on the back of the farmers and producers, profits are generated which only harm the farmers.
Everyone can think for themselves how much high-quality food is worth to them and how much they are willing to pay for it.

Crimes

Could such a currency changeover reduce the number of crimes? All crimes committed out of greed, which I would count all economic crimes as well, rather not.

But if a stable monetary system succeeds in relieving the burden on the poorer sections of the population, improving their position and giving them prospects for a better future, I could imagine that a reduction in crime is possible.

One thing that would certainly decrease would be wars, as they would no longer be financially sustainable.

What other problems have been solved?

By using different cryptocurrencies in the various regions, we have solved a problem of the gold standard. As all monetary systems used to be covered by the same value, namely gold, problems arose with import and export. For example, if the imported goods were paid for with dollars, the exporting country, for example France, could always exchange the received dollars for gold at a fixed exchange rate. As a result, France was able to print more banknotes, since it now had additional gold from America, and America had to collect banknotes to ensure that the dollar was 100% covered.

With crypto-currencies this does not happen any more because each cryptocurrency is covered by itself.

As mentioned above, there is also no reason why some form of cash should not become established. For example, 10% of the respective cryptocurrency could be used as cash. But the issuing of cash must also be transparent and visible to everyone, the only way to prevent more than the 10% from circulating as cash and thus inflation. The supply of cash can basically be carried out by anyone, no state is needed. This used to work with gold coins and would work again now. The verification and production of cash can easily be mapped on a blockchain.

Lead currency

At the beginning of Part 3 of this book I talked about a reserve currency in the form of Bitcoin and in the following chapters I completely ignored Bitcoin. I have not forgotten it, I just wanted to install local cryptocurrencies first and show the possible effects.

First, we need to take a brief look at the requirements that such a reserve or trade currency must meet.

Such a cryptocurrency must be stable. Price jumps of several percent in a few days, as is currently the case with real Bitcoin, must not happen. We could achieve this by linking this cryptocurrency to all other existing currencies. Similar to a shopping basket as used to determine inflation. Only this shopping cart does not contain any goods, but all crypto-currencies in equal shares. This makes our trading currency, we call it Bitcoin, stable.

Another possibility would be to link it to the gold price, which would also keep the price stable. Whether one of these two options, or even another, will prevail, I cannot say. I just wanted to point out two possible approaches.

What else must our Bitcoin be capable of? It must allow high transaction speeds. A transaction, no matter where, must be completed in a matter of minutes.

The number of transactions per second is also essential. If the Bitcoin is to be used as a world trade currency, several hundred thousand transactions per second must be possible. As already mentioned several times, the real Bitcoin can't do this, but a cryptocurrency based on a DAG (Directed Acyclic Graph) can easily do this.

Of course, this trading currency must run on a public and transparent network. In this way, we create a worldwide observation possibility by the individual participants.

These are the basic characteristics that a world trading currency must have.

Let us now set up a model of how such a trading currency could work:

All imports and exports are paid for with Bitcoin. Bitcoin is traded on decentralized exchanges and can be exchanged into any cryptocurrency. This creates a free market that cannot be controlled by anyone. It is therefore up to each region whether it holds Bitcoin or only exchanges Bitcoin when it is needed.

As the Bitcoin is paid with its own cryptocurrency, excessive hoarding of Bitcoins by the individual regions can be excluded. This is because if a region or country hoards huge amounts of Bitcoin, it means that in return there is not enough of its own cryptocurrency and the region has no liquid funds available.

However, there could still be two extreme situations that need to be treated.

One is countries that import only and export nothing. The second is the opposite, countries that only export and import nothing.

How do we deal with these situations?

Let us first look at the countries or regions that only import. They would have to exchange their cryptocurrency for Bitcoin all the time to be able to pay for the imports. This would mean that, in the worst case, they would no longer have their own crypto coins available and would therefore no longer be able to make payments in their own country. This in no way affects the coverage of their currency, which is still there, just not in their country.

On the other hand, we would have the exporting countries that would have plenty of Bitcoins available and, in extreme cases, would already have all their own crypto coins in their region.

Since Bitcoin is only used as a trading currency, these countries would be sitting on Bitcoins that they could not use and would therefore be dead capital.

Another problem that could arise is a rise in the price of Bitcoin because these Bitcoins are not on the market, Bitcoin could become more expensive. This is based on the simple principle of supply and demand. However, if Bitcoin becomes more expensive, exports could suffer as the goods become too expensive. Therefore, each exporting country will try to get rid of the Bitcoins as soon as possible and thereby not increase the Bitcoin price unnecessarily.

One solution could provide the oldest money in the world, gold.
We use a cryptocurrency called Aurum, which is backed up 100% with physical gold. Only bars and coins may be used for the deposit. Jewellery and gold processed in devices may not be used for deposit.

What is the point of such a gold-backed cryptocurrency now?

One would now have the possibility to exchange Bitcoins for gold. As exporting countries need gold for their production of smartphones, medical devices, computers or other electronic equipment, they would thus have the possibility to invest their surplus Bitcoins in a sensible way and thus prevent price increases of Bitcoin.
However, it must be noted that aurumcoins are immediately destroyed when gold is used to manufacture electronic components. Only in this way can the 100% coverage be maintained. This process can also easily be carried out via a blockchain and monitored by anyone in the world.

The question now is, what do the importing countries get out of it?

The importing countries now have the opportunity to obtain gold by recycling their old imported equipment.

When they melt down the recycled gold into coins or bars, new aurum coins are created, which can be exchanged for Bitcoin.

This would be one way of establishing a circular economy in international trade.

Since this model is intended as a basis for discussion, it is far from perfect. It cannot and should not be. It is intended to stimulate the imagination.

But we can see that there are certainly possibilities to set up such a system, but it remains questionable whether the existing elites are interested in it. I do not believe that this would mean a loss of power that the elites would not accept without a fight.

By no means all problems solved

On the previous pages I have tried to sketch a possible solution, knowing that this only covers a small part. It should have become clear that a cryptocurrency or a currency covered by a cryptocurrency could already reduce or even solve some problems.

The approach I have outlined should stimulate discussion. As many people as possible should take part in this discussion, not only specialists and experts, no, lay people and unbiased fellow citizens must also contribute their views. As I have already mentioned several times, a change of system must come from the population, which means that as many people as possible must be involved and work together.

Freedom requires commitment and personal responsibility, but rewards us with independence and the realization of our chosen lifestyle.

But this requires a much-needed rethink among the population, as I have already explained in the section on social problems.

If we go down this road, it will not be easy and some would find such radical changes hard to bear. I have no illusions about that. There will be a lot of company bankruptcies and many unemployed as a result. The worst thing is that the poorer sections of the population would again be hit hardest. Those who are actually least to blame for the whole mess. But a change of system would at least bring about an improvement. There would be a light at the end of the tunnel, even if not immediately, it will take time for an improvement, but it will come.

As already mentioned, a covered monetary system does not solve all the problems by a long way, but it would be a way of making the world a better place. Again, of course, there is a side effect, in that by solving some problems there would be more resources available to solve the remaining problems.

But until that happens, a few other challenges need to be addressed. More on this in the next chapter.

Continuative technologies

Currently, the handling, sending, storage and use of cryptocurrencies is anything but user-friendly. It is necessary to develop connection technologies that raise the handling to the level of debit or credit cards.

Fortunately, there are already some projects on the market that promote exactly these aspects of applicability. Meanwhile, it is possible to avoid the long, hexadecimal wallet addresses and use clear names when sending cryptocurrencies. It is also possible to send different crypto-currencies to one clear name address, the allocation to the respective wallets (BTC, LTC, ETH, etc.) is done automatically.

The pioneers of this technology are Unstoppable Domains, Ethereum Name Service and Celsius Network. These three providers make it possible, among other things, to send different cryptocurrencies to clear name addresses.

On the merchant side, Ingenico (the market leader in payment terminals) and SALAMANTEX in the area of payment at the checkout. SALAMANTEX provides the software solution and Ingenico the terminals.

There are signs of progress in the field of connection technologies to shift the problems of handling cryptocurrencies towards mass suitability.

Another problem of the adaptation is the connection of real data, such as conventional bank accounts, weather data etc., with the blockchain applications. From a purely technical point of view, a wide variety of transactions can be automated on a blockchain. To achieve this, there are so-called smart contracts on various blockchains. A Smartcontract in its simplest form is nothing more than an IF/THEN logic.

Meaning:

If a previously determined event, e.g. an incoming payment, occurs, an action is automatically carried out, e.g. the goods are dispatched.

With Smartcontracts, for example, it is also possible to control more complex processes. These could be real estate transactions, for example. The buyer decides on a property, the data is automatically forwarded to his bank, as soon as the bank has approved the financing, a purchase contract is drawn up, the purchase amount is transferred to an escrow account, etc., until the land register entry is finally confirmed.

All these processes can, from a purely technical point of view, be fully automated and can replace notaries and lawyers almost completely.

But this creates at least two problems:

The first is the programming of the respective smart contracts.

For small IF/THEN contracts there are already platforms on which you can build Smartcontracts without any programming knowledge. But if you want to build more complex contracts, you have to work carefully because every little mistake can lead to the deposited credit disappearing forever or rather being sent to a place from where it can no longer be retrieved.

The second problem is the communication with data from the real world. So, how do I get access to my bank account It all sounds relatively simple, but it does have some dangers. How can you verify, i.e. confirm that this data is correct at all, is it the right bank account and is it really in the possession of the right person? Of course, this is confirmed by the bank at present, but in the future such intermediaries / brokers should be replaced, as they represent a single point of failure. If the bank manager has a bad day, he can stop or at least delay a transfer at any time and this is exactly what needs to be avoided.

If we look at the example of the purchase of real estate, we see that we need some external data for this smart contract. Starting with the buyer's data, the seller's data, the data in the land register and many more in between. All this data must be 100% correct and verified.

We see that already when buying a property a lot of real world data is needed to make a smart contract work properly. Imagine how much data is required when selling a whole company.

Another, let's say, sub-problem lies in the possibility of block-chain-spanning communication.

As an example again our house purchase:

My municipality stores the population data on the Ethereum blockchain, the land registry uses a private blockchain from Hyperledger/Linux and the seller's municipality uses a Cardano blockchain. Again, we see the problems that arise and need to be solved.

But I can reassure you at this point, these problems have been known for some time and some companies are taking care of exactly these problems. As the probably best known among several, Chainlink should be mentioned here. Chainlink allows you to access real world data, to check and verify the quality of the data, and to communicate with all kinds of blockchains.

But a lot more needs to be done in this direction to increase acceptance among the population.

Clarification of Fact

It is not only the technical aspects that lead to greater acceptance. The educational work is important. A negative basic attitude towards the cryptocurrencies prevails among the population. States and mainstream media have made a major contribution to this negative attitude. Nearly every article in newspapers and magazines deals with illegal activities in connection with Bitcoin and Co. Darknet activities, cybercrime, financing of terror and money laundering are published with great pleasure and contribute the major part to the negative image of the cryptocurrencies.

Unfortunately, this form of reporting is very one-sided and is all too often written by unsuspecting or uninformed journalists who do not take the trouble to research and publish real facts.

It is true that crypto-currencies are used for illegal activities, but the impression is created that crypto-currencies are used in all criminal activities. This would imply that there was no illegal business before 2009, as the cryptocurrencies did not exist yet.

It is true that crypto-currencies are used in criminal activities, but the proportion is negligible if one takes the sums moved by banks as a comparison.

Why do you think that the offices of the Deutsche Bank have been searched several times by judicial officers and countless fines in millions and billions have been imposed? Why are cash couriers picked up almost daily at the border crossings of the USA and Mexico?

These are only two examples that have nothing to do with cryptocurrencies and are by far not the only ones.

Cryptocurrencies are the same as the euro, dollar, franc and all other currencies, they are used for illegal transactions, but these illegal transactions are far from being the main part of the applications. The main use of any currency is to pay for goods and services, whether these are crypto or national currencies.

Another argument that is often cited is the immense power consumption of Bitcoin. It is absolutely correct that the Bitcoin network has a huge power consumption. However, it is regularly concealed that the Bitcoin network is 75% covered by renewable sources. It also completely ignores the fact that the server farms of the banks and the bank buildings also require energy. All the computers, air conditioning, lighting and other systems in the banks do not run on air and love, but consume huge amounts of energy. If we now assume, purely hypothetically, that the banks will be replaced by Bitcoin, the energy problem should be solved.

Another aspect of energy consumption is also completely ignored. The high energy consumption only occurs with cryptocurrencies that use the proof of work mechanism, Bitcoin, Litecoin, Ethereum, to name but a few.

The majority of cryptocurrencies use the Proof of Stake, Proof of Capacity, Proof of Burn or Delegated Proof of Stake mechanism.

All these mechanisms are much less energy intensive than the Proof of Work. It is also the case that Ethereum Blockchain is already working on a switch to Proof of Stake.

Similarly, Bitcoin is working on the Lightning network to outsource transactions from the Bitcoin Blockchain, which should increase transaction speed and reduce power consumption.

We see the crypto-currencies are often put in a bad light, without going into detail about the connections. At least one unpleasant question arises from this: "Who profits from these negative representations"?

To find the answer, we try the following approach: "Follow the money."

Who has the most to lose when crypto-currencies prevail? The simple answer, governments, central banks and commercial banks. Governments lose control over their currencies and thus control over the population and the economy. In addition, they would become increasingly dependent on the population and their constantly bubbling sources of income would dry up. The central banks would face a similar problem, their power over national currencies would be lost and sometimes their raison d'être seriously threatened. The same applies to commercial banks, whose purpose in its present form would be lost.

It stands to reason that these institutions will do their utmost to avoid changing the current situation. Unfortunately, it is also significant that this behaviour will have serious consequences in the foreseeable future.

The one example that impressively reflects this behaviour is KODAK. KODAK was the world market leader in the analogue film and photo industry, but failed to keep up with technical progress. The digitalization of the film and photo industry was smiled at and dismissed as a short-lived trend that had no future. KODAK plunged from world market leader to irrelevance in a few years, simply because KODAK was too secure and arrogant to adapt to progress.

A similar fate befell the music industry in the late 1990s. Even the record labels of the music giants thought themselves untouchable and lost sight of reality completely. Then came NAPSTER! Three guys developed a system for sharing music over the internet, which caused a slump in record and CD sales. Apple did the rest. The music industry was simply overwhelmed by progress and, due to its arrogance, completely missed the boat. Today we listen to music via streaming services such as Spotify or Applemusic. Ariola, His Masters Voice, Polyphon, RCA and many more, nobody knows them anymore, before NAPSTER they were giants of the music industry.

Yes, now back to the topic.

Very often the sheer amount of cryptocurrencies and blockchain applications is also criticized. In my opinion, this is completely justified, and I am sure that about 90% of the currently existing cryptocurrencies and blockchain applications will disappear. This can have many reasons, for example no real benefit, bad implementation or there is a better application for the same problem, the reasons can be many.

The free market and thus the users will decide what stays and what goes, that's the way it has to be.

Last but not least

With this book I have tried to show the genesis of money. From the beginnings to a possible future. I have tried to explain the inadequacies and resulting injustices of today's currencies and have created a vision of the future.

I hope I was able to reach some people who have not yet dealt with the matter and maybe I have aroused their curiosity for further research.

We are currently experiencing the Corona crisis, in which almost the entire world was shut down. Many people are sitting at home and, justifiably, are worried about their future. Governments and central banks are shooting out of all pipes and flooding the world with new dollars, euros and francs, to name but a few. This unbelievable amount of newly printed money should once again solve all the problems. If you have made it this far by reading it, you should realize for yourself that this will go badly wrong and that the poorer sections of the population will once again be allowed to pay the bill.

In the coming weeks and months we will see company bankruptcies, unemployment and bankrupt states. We will also see new laws and regulations being introduced under the guise of the crisis to better monitor and "protect" the population. In the end, when everything goes down the drain, the politicians and experts who are responsible for the chaos will look for culprits to justify their own actions. They will desperately cling to their sinecures and do everything to keep their power.

I hope that nobody believes them anymore and that everyone realizes that they have been fooled for years.

Let us use this crisis together to make a difference, even if it is only small steps.

> *"A journey of a thousand miles begins with a single step"*
>
> *Lao Tse*

I wish you all the best, stay healthy and take care of each other.

Further reading

Ludwig von Mises
Human Action

Murray N. Rothbard
What hast he Government done to our Money

Friedrich A. Hayek
The Road to Serfdom

G. Edward Griffin
The Creature from Jekyll Island

Daniel Drescher
Blockchain Basics

Andreas M. Antonopoulos
The Internet of Money

Glossary

Bitcoin
Blockchain based cryptocurrency. The concept was presented in late 2008 and went online in 2009. Inventor Satoshi Nakamoto. The Bitcoin network could not be attacked until today. Bitcoin Core is the oldest and first public blockchain worldwide.

Bitpanda
Austrian Crypto Exchange with headquarters in Vienna

Bison
German crypto exchange based in Stuttgart

BIS
Bank for International Settlements with headquarters in Basel. The BIS is the central bank of the central banks.

Blockchain
Decentralized computer network. Transactions take place directly between sender and receiver. All network participants have the same rights. The network is tamper-proof and does not require a control authority.

Blockstack
Blockstack offers a decentralized digital identity. The deposited data is stored on the blockchain. Based on this system there are countless applications on the market that can be used with this identity. When logging into an application, the data is read cryptographically and cannot be stored by the application. The data always remains with the owner. One identity for many applications.

BRAVE Browser
Internet browser that does not pass on data and pays the user with BAT (Basic Attention Token) when viewing content.

Chainlink
Enables blockchain spanning transactions and the connection of real world data, such as bank accounts or weather data

CBDC
Central bank digital Currency.
Digital fiat currency issued directly by central banks and has nothing to do with cryptocurrencies.

Coinbase
Crypto exchange based in London

DAG
Directed Acyclic Graph. A DAG is a network that spreads like a directed spider web. To execute a transaction, the sender must first confirm two other transactions. It is also based on mathematics and cryptography, but theoretically can carry out an infinite number of transactions per second. HEDERA Hashgraph and MIOTA use a DAG.

Deflation
Revaluation of a currency. This results in falling prices.

DuckDuckgo
Internet search engine that does not collect or share data.

ENS
Ethereum Name Service is an application on the Ethereum Blockchain that allows you to convert wallet addresses into clear names. Behind dezentrale.eth there is an Ethereum, a Bitcoin and a Litecoin Wallet. All wallets are controlled by the clear name.

ECB
European Central Bank with headquarters in Frankfurt. Independent central bank, issues the euro and ensures price stability in the euro countries.

Frontpage
Internet search engine that does not collect or share data.

Gold
Aurum/ Au precious metal that has been used as money for over 6000 years. Third best electrical conductor of all metals. Does not react with oxygen and acids (virtually stainless).

Inflation
Expanding the currency volume and thereby devaluing the currency. This always results in rising prices.

Ingenico
World market leader for payment terminals. Enables payment with ATM and credit cards. Now also cryptocurrencies with the SALAMANTEX software.

Napster
A decentralized network where music could be downloaded directly from sender to receiver. The central server only served as a table of contents and showed where which music data was stored.

Cryptocurrency
A currency that runs on a blockchain or DAG. It cannot be influenced from the outside and does not require an external control authority.

Proof of Burn
When a transaction is confirmed, coins are burned. This creates a value in the blockchain, making it secure. Anyone who wants to manipulate the transactions would have to destroy a large number of their own coins to confirm the manipulated transactions.

Proof of Stake
Each network participant who wants to confirm transactions must deposit their own coins as security. If a participant manipulates transactions, he loses all his deposited coins.

Proof of Work
Every network participant who confirms a block in a blockchain must first solve a computationally intensive mathematical puzzle. Electrical energy is required due to the necessary computing power. Due to the expensive electrical energy a manipulation is almost impossible. If data should be changed afterwards, all mathematical puzzles that were calculated after the manipulated transaction would have to be recalculated. So fast that no other network participant notices.

SALAMANTEX
A payment service provider that enables merchants to accept cryptocurrencies for payment. The merchant has no exchange rate risk as the exchange rates are fetched during the payment process and are only valid for 35 seconds. SALAMANTEX is an Austrian company and is certified by the Financial Market Authority.

Smartcontract

Smart contract that runs on a blockchain. A Smartcontract can execute complex processes autonomously. In its simplest form a Smartcontract is an if/ then Logic. If a defined event occurs, then a defined action is triggered.

Unstoppable domains

UD also offers clear name addresses. dezentrale.zil and dezentrale.crypto are linked to different wallets and enable transactions with clear names. Via UD it is also possible to publish entire websites in a censorship-resistant manner.

Wallet

The digital purse in which, for example, Bitcoin is stored.

WIREX

Visa card with connected crypto wallets that can be used at all Visa acceptance points worldwide.

Sources

Information on economic and other data

www. haushaltssteuerung.com/government debt-europe-ranking.html#government debt-gdp

www. world.en/economy/article167215622/Zombie-companies-sustain-the-risk-of-a-new-crisis.html

www. bundesbank.com/en/tasks

www. goldsilber.org/true-inflation.php

www. finanzfinder24.en/the-real-inflation/

www. ecb.europa.eu/home/search/html/index.en.html?q=money supply+m3

www. mytoday.at/sva-contributions-and-liability insurance-in-austria/

www. eu-info.com/euro-monetary union/5011/5353/5992/

www. gold.com/cash/

ec.europa.eu/info/consultations/eu-initiative-restrictions-payments-cash_en

www.handelsblatt.com/meinung/gastbeitraege/gastkomme ntar-ezb-chefin-lagarde-wir-werden-alles-tun-um-den-euro-raum-zu-stuetzen/25661362.html?ticket=ST-1223215-Z0RfJ3txlBdskCsnY4Xu-ap5
en.wikipedia.org/wiki/PersC3%B6nlichkeitsrecht_(Germany)

Disclaimer

All contents are for your information and have been compiled to the best of our knowledge and belief.

The contents of this book do not in any way constitute investment advice or investment recommendations. Any investment may result in the loss of the assets invested. Contact a financial expert before making any investment.

None of the proposed measures is intended to incite unlawful behaviour. Before implementing measures, find out about the legal situation in your country.

Contact

d.mueller(at)dezentrale.at

www. dezentrale.at

YouTube: dezentrale at